# THE
# MOON
# DUST
# DREAM
*Dictionary*

Unlock the True Meanings of Your Dreams
with the Wisdom of the Moon

## FLORANCE SAUL

**The Moon Dust Dream Dictionary**
Florance Saul

First published in the UK and USA in 2023 by
Watkins, an imprint of Watkins Media Limited
Unit 11, Shepperton House, 83–93 Shepperton Road
London N1 3DF

enquiries@watkinspublishing.com

Commissioning Editor: Ella Chappell
Assistant Editor: Brittany Willis
Head of Design: Karen Smith
Cover Designer: Francesca Corsini
Interior Designer: Kieryn Tyler
Production: Uzma Taj

A CIP record for this book is available from the British Library

ISBN: 978-1-78678-743-9 (Paperback)
ISBN: 978-1-78678-744-6 (eBook)

10 9 8 7 6 5 4 3 2 1

Printed in China

www.watkinspublishing.com

To access exclusive spiritual
content visit: auntyflo.com/
moon and use the code:
beautifulmoon

# Contents

# Part One

# Introduction

# About This Book

When I was a young girl, I used to keep a dream diary. I was fascinated by the seemingly real – and usually surreal – experiences that flooded my awareness after falling asleep. I believed "the night" was a doorway into another dimension. It was as if the moon was talking to me in a language I almost-but-didn't-quite understand. So, I kept a journal. And while my friends studied French, maths or dance, my interests steered me in a very different direction.

For as long as I can remember, I have strived to discover where my mind travels at night and divine the messages my dreams contain. Of course, in our empirical world, we can talk of nerve networks, the hormones serotonin and melatonin or the science of sleep and identify what is happening on a chemical level. We can also explore psychological perspectives and the underlying causes of our emotions. But for some reason, this analytical approach to seeking the "what" of dreams never seemed to satisfy my mystical curiosity to understand the "why" and the "where".

I began to delve, open-minded and open-hearted, into the exploration of mysticism. And while I faced the inevitable pushback from the boisterous, bragging empiricist (in myself and others), the more subtle realm of mysticism innately made more sense to me. I stayed focused, knowing that just because books hadn't been written on the subject I was pursuing didn't mean they never would be.

We all know that a long walk in nature can bring us peace, creativity or elusive answers. We have an innate belief in this fact, but can we explain it? Not really. It was this innate belief that kept me digging for something more tangible.

It may be that one day we will have solid scientific explanations for what we currently call mysticism, and I am open to that. But for now, I remain committed to the idea that just because we can't explain it doesn't mean it doesn't exist.

## BELIEF SYSTEMS

I believe that it is essential to recognize that we all have different belief systems. An important part of any belief system is the lexicon – the vocabulary – used to label what are often shared human experiences. Conversely, we can sometimes clam up when met with words that fall outside of that lexicon, despite them describing these shared traits.

The most obvious example of this is the word "God". How we define "God" will either unite us, pit us against each other or simply turn us off. Yet, in our hearts, most of us have ways to tap into something bigger than ourselves, such as meditating, taking deep breaths when we are stressed, counting to ten before we respond angrily, or even simply wishing each other "good luck" etc. Iconography and cultural manifestations may vary, but as far as I am concerned, these all tap into the same thing.

Likewise with mysticism. Call it what you will – intuition, a sixth sense, sub-conscious perception – it is all the same.

In this book, I will have to commit to one lexicon or another. So, I am going to use my own. But before I do, I will try to deconstruct some of the barriers that may block the otherwise aligned of us, so we are not derailed by what are essentially different-coloured Post-It notes on shared human experiences.

We may be looking at the same things, just with different labels. I would like to establish early in this book that when we look, we may share the same feelings if not the same words to describe them. The following sections attempt to define common ground – a common belief system – despite our various backgrounds. I want us to find a common lexicon in our efforts to help us better interpret the meanings of our dreams.

## LOOKING BACK

I will go into greater detail in the following chapters, but for now, I want to introduce the idea of tapping into the wisdom of our ancestors.

Our culture often refers to the legacies of scientific thought leaders such as Darwin, Einstein, Freud, Newton etc. Human history is rich with pioneering ideas on which we build our ever-evolving and increasingly sophisticated cultures.

This set of thought leaders isn't limited to recent scientific experimenters. The wheel is the perfect example of ancient engineering that got it right. Greek mathematicians and philosophers put their stamp on the intellectual world in profound ways, Rome and Egypt contributed immensely, and the list goes on. From mathematical proofs to complex engineering, irrigation, navigation, the arts, and even democratic processes, the legal system and the way we think, the wisdom of the ancients can be found in every branch of academia. And that's not all.

In addition to the wisdom of the ancients that we _do_ understand, there is wisdom that we _don't_ yet understand; mysterious advancements that somehow got lost in the dusts of time yet are no less tangible than the wheel. The Pyramids of Egypt continue to baffle contemporary engineers. How these were built with such accuracy without the aid of modern tools and planning software remains a mystery. The Nazca Lines carved in the Peruvian desert by the Incas an enigma, elegant and enormous iconography impossible to view unless from an altitude the Incas themselves couldn't have gained. Like the Pyramids, these lines defy explanation.

While the feats of the Pyramids and the Nazca Lines are remarkable enough, their mystery doesn't stop at their engineering. Both have mystical, spiritual or astronomical components to their design that show how these cultures dedicated extraordinary resources to honouring their cultural beliefs.

And so it was with the Mesopotamian culture, too.

I have a deep personal interest in what are known as the Clay Tablets of Babylon: a vast collection of carved clay tablets that date back 3,700 years but were only recently discovered. These tablets contain, among other things, the world's oldest and most accurate trigonometric tables used in the construction of palaces, temples and canals. These mathematical documents pre-date the Greeks by 1,000 years and have rewritten the history of progressive thinking.

Another component of the ancient wisdom unearthed with the discovery of these tablets is what is considered to be the earliest explorations into astronomy, astrology and dream interpretation. While many of these tablets have yet to be translated, what is already known about this branch of mysticism is proving to be no less profound than the tablets' mathematics.

## LOOKING FORWARD

These tablets are kept, for the most part, in the British Museum, not far from where I used to work. I discovered them for myself one lunch hour in 2009 and became immediately mesmerized by the voice inside them trying to speak out.

From that day, I spent every lunch hour in their presence, and so began my 15-year journey here. I read up and immersed myself in the translations, culture, interpretations and wisdom. I felt such a connection that I wanted to spread the word about their dream interpretations.

Initially, I chose to format my interpretations in a contemporary way. I steered clear of referencing the clay tablets, fearing it would be too esoteric, too out there, or too soon for casual dreamers. But since I launched my website for dream interpretations, it has seen over 100 million visitors seeking deeper meaning and finding inspiration, shattering any preconceptions I had of the resonance others would feel about this information. It has been so widely enjoyed that I now wish to open the doors to the source material behind the work that has led me here – the Clay Tablets of Babylon, as these clearly connect to a deep and very real place in the human psyche.

I will refer to these tablets, and the wisdom of the Mesopotamians, many times in this book. It is often said that we stand on the shoulders of giants, and this is true. The Mesopotamians are newly rediscovered giants.

## LOOKING UP

The other key component of this book relates to the moon and its phases. The moon is arguably the most extraordinary heavenly body in our human experience. Some may say that the sun is more extraordinary, but I beg to differ.

The sun is the norm and our common experience. Plus, it is impossible to look at. We don't look directly at the sun; we look at the sky, the clouds, the earth and our fellow humans. I often feel that, emotionally, we accept the sun as our default state. In the same way that it can be fun to consider whether or not a fish is aware that it is in water, I believe that daylight is the medium within which we go about our daily lives and is less interesting for that reason. As life-giving and ubiquitous as air, the sun has little intrigue and is not as "sexy" as the moon.

After the splendour of sunset and the plunging of our lives into darkness, we become less outgoing and more sensitive, hyperaware of any dangers that may lie in the shadows. This nocturnal world is illuminated by the extraordinary heavenly body that glides over us each night, hundreds of thousands of times brighter than the average star.

What must our ancestors have thought of such beauty and mystery? That is actually a rhetorical question. The Babylonian clay tablets tell us precisely what they thought. I haven't yet met a person who has claimed that they have never gazed at the moon in wonder. It is a beacon and a Siren song; it casts a spell on us and has inspired scientists and artists, mystics and adventurers for as long as humans have been curious.

Let us not fall into the conceit of thinking we know all there is to know about the effects of the moon on the human psyche. We have evolved – and continue to evolve – under the constant influence and watchful light of this unique, mesmerizing orb. How can it not guide us, conscious or otherwise?

Just as butterflies, birds and whales navigate the globe using sensitivities beyond our understanding; just as the animal kingdom is known to seek higher ground prior to tsunamis, again, using sensitivities beyond our understanding; we too have innate sensitivities. It would be foolish to assume otherwise and be more appropriate to trust and believe in our talents.

This book delves a little deeper into how we innately interpret the lunar phases and acknowledges that these interpretations must, in some way, inform our subconscious. I don't shy away from believing such things are real. I ask that you remain open to the fact that, while we may operate on a highly progressive conscious level, it is entirely plausible that this is just the tip of our cerebral iceberg and that mysticism, however we define it, is part of the human psyche.

## IN CONCLUSION

While this book is intended to be a fun, well-considered dream dictionary, I will be referencing esoteric material and subtle influences that aren't openly embraced in our culture.

The following chapters go into greater detail about the past and the moon. If you have made it this far, I encourage you to dig a little deeper so that when you are using the dictionary for quick reference, the interpretations are more meaningful for you.

We don't need to reinvent the wheel. If we can familiarize ourselves with the wealth of wisdom in dream interpretation and the lunar phases detailed by the giants that came before us, we can embark upon a more meaningful and rewarding journey toward deeper self-awareness.

# About Ishtar

Few things fascinate us more than our dreams – if we can remember them, that is. Dreams can be bewildering, surreal, powerful and confusing, and it isn't uncommon to hear our friends talk over coffee about the wild visions they had while asleep and for us to try to divine their meaning.

We are not the first generation to be curious about dream interpretation. Throughout history, countless cultures have sought to make sense of this parallel existence of our dream self. Until science can answer every mystical question – which it has yet to do – we should remain open to all avenues of information in our pursuit of meaning.

Indeed, science hasn't just failed to satisfy all our questions. Worse, it has intimidated subtler forms of intuition and sullied well-trodden spiritual paths. The mere presence of the scientific method, even as it fails to provide answers, often bullies our mind – or our culture – into dismissing the gaps in our logical understanding as simply "soon to be explained".

"God of the gaps" is a theological perspective in which gaps in scientific knowledge are taken to be evidence or proof of God's existence. Of course, as science looks further up into the sky and down into the atom, those gaps get smaller. The empiricist's argument is that as the gaps get smaller, so does God.

I see it differently.

Gaps are where the light comes in, and the more we shore up those gaps, the less we can see through them. This idea that any gap is simply "soon to be explained" belittles the genius of the past visionaries, cultures and gurus who devoted themselves to the same pursuit of meaning we are committed to, except without a lab coat and safety goggles obscuring their view.

Richard Feynman, a co-recipient of the 1965 Nobel Prize in theoretical physics, famously said, "It is a poor poet who falls silent upon finding out that the sun is actually a massive sphere of hydrogen fusing into helium." I would venture to say that of course the poor poet fell silent. Let the scientist wax prosaic of its chemistry, and let the poet wax lyrical of its warmth.

There is more to life than three dimensions and a few fundamental forces. There is more to the mind than a trillion nerve cells firing. There is more to our life experience than everything we import through our five senses. The more we look back in time, to when empirical "gaps" were less clogged with uninspired prose, the more we can find individuals, cultures and civilizations compelled to the study not of dark matter but of light, not of helium but of Helios, not of dream homes and dream jobs but of the dreams themselves.

If we are genuinely interested in delving into our subconscious to divine the meanings of our dreams, we can do worse than spending a little time studying civilizations that devoted themselves to the art of dream interpretation, taking these visions more seriously than perhaps our friends may do.

History provides us with a treasure trove of insight that we can access while pursuing meaning and inspiration. We should listen to our elders and, if necessary, retell their findings, even if that means modernizing the format and updating the language in which we do so.

The following pages offer a brief introduction to the sources, cultures and civilizations of the past that I feel are particularly relevant to the subject matter at hand. They pioneered deep dives into the world of dream interpretation and I gained insight and inspiration from them.

## MESOPOTAMIA

In the location of modern-day Iraq and dating back 5,000 years, Mesopotamia is regarded as the first great civilization. Having "inspired some of the most important developments in human history, including the invention of the wheel, the planting of the first cereal crops, and the development of cursive script, mathematics, astronomy and agriculture",[1] the region produced the first documentation of human intellectual and academic progress.

Mesopotamia was composed of four distinct peoples – Sumerians, Assyrians, Babylonians and Akkadians. Each one brought new ideas into the sphere of human awareness, producing the first recorded philosophers, and their influence can't be overstated.

Conversely, much of their pioneering work can't be fully understood either. As they looked skyward, seeking to understand their purpose and man's place in the universe, they projected that reverence upon all their terrestrial arc. It is known that their study of the stars, the movement of the heavenly bodies and the rhythm of the skies informed much of their architectural design. Yet we still don't understand precisely how the pyramids were conceived, planned and built. Nor are we aware of the reasoning behind these temples' extraordinarily accurate alignment with the stars. *How* they did this is one thing; *Why* they did it is another.

One needs only to scratch the surface of the mysteries of such epic creations to realize that their design must have tapped into information millennia ahead of its time. The Mesopotamians were clearly on to something. We don't yet understand the full extent of their wisdom, and it would be foolish of us to dismiss it offhand.

The region's passion for mathematics and astronomy as predictive sciences, medicine, human wellbeing and the cultivation of theology led naturally to interests in astrology, the heavens and the zodiac, mysticism and dream interpretation.

And this is where it gets fascinating.

---

1 Milton-Edwards, Beverley, "Iraq, past, present and future: a thoroughly-modern mandate?", *History and Policy*, Vol 19, May 2003, pp74–82

## THE CLAY TABLETS OF THE SUMERIANS

Sumerians were pioneers of the written word and provided us with the first historical scribed documents. Cuneiform characters were carved into wet clay using a reed stylus and dried or fired into stone, and many of the resulting clay tablets survived for millennia.

Buried in the dusts of time and overlooked by marauding civilizations, 15,000 of these clay tablets – these windows to the minds of the past – were discovered in the 1850s and translated for the modern world.

While their messages may seem antiquated, quaint and inconceivably distant from our Google generation, the content provides an encyclopaedic insight for those prepared to listen.

Their documentation of dream interpretation and astrology is the earliest evidence on the matter in recorded history. It outlines how the Mesopotamian civilization had a deep respect and belief that dreams had predictive qualities. Through studying these tablets, we've learned that the Sumerians often slept in sacred places and performed rituals to their dream goddess, Ishtar, all for the purpose of encountering prophetic dreams. This advanced culture went to extraordinary lengths to summon dreams and harness their messages. And this was no passing trend; this practice was honoured and revered for thousands of years.

Throughout this book, I will be referencing these Sumerian clay tablets to add deep historical support and credibility to the interpretations of our most frequent contemporary dream subjects.

## THE BABYLONIAN ZODIAC STARGATE

The other pioneering civilization of the Mesopotamian region that I want to discuss is that of the Babylonians.

Babylonians were keen astronomers, charting the first accurate maps of the skies and pondering the original big astronomical and astrological questions. They were the first to describe constellations and astrology through myths and define the 12 zodiacal signs. Though refined by the Egyptians and then shaped into its current form by the Greeks, the Babylonian system of astrology was seeded 5,000 years ago and has influenced our species ever since then.

This process began with grouping stars into "constellations"; most significantly, in the North, Cassiopeia, Pleiades and the Great Bear, and in the South, the Southern Cross. Through studying the motion of the stars and planets in relation to the moon and sun, they developed calculations of the lunation – the exact duration of the lunar cycle – and learned to predict eclipses. This is a remarkable achievement considering the rudimentary science available at the time. Science wasn't the driving force behind understanding the motions of the heavens. For them, omens, mysticism, wellbeing, gratitude and worship were the soul's currency.

Remember: while modern humans have been on earth for approximately 200,000 years, modern science only dates back about 200 years. For 99.9 per cent of our time on earth, we have tuned into mysticism for guidance. This science experiment we are currently conducting is intoxicating and compelling and in its infancy. It is like a new toy or a new friend, a gadget that fascinates. For comparison, that is two weeks in the life of a 40-year-old. One wouldn't expect a middle-aged man to turn his back on his entire life's experience based on a two-week read of a paperback, no matter how gripping it may be. Nor should we be too hasty to put down the intangible mysticism that is so intractable from our development as a species.

Mysticism is in our DNA, and the Babylonians knew that in spirit and pursued its meaning with fervour. They mapped the stars, watched the planets, defined the zodiac into "Houses of the Moon" and projected this data onto human existence, tracing ways to use the heavens to inspire a better life on earth.

In the context of astrology, astronomical predictions were used to compile omens. They didn't consider planets as gods but rather as messages. The moon's movement was measured, eclipses were graded by colour and brightness, and the messages were documented, interpreted and applied to a civilization that became dominant in the world thousands of years ahead of its time.

We are still left with many unanswered questions. What is clear is that the Babylonians invested a great deal in astrology and it served them well. They also mastered the art of dream interpretation based on lunar energy. They believed the orbits of the planets are one with our existence and hold power to guide, inform and inspire our fate. It is this, the true essence of astrology, that explores the relationship between celestial activity and human behaviour.

The most potent celestial body – after the sun, of course, which guides our days – is the moon, which guides our nights.

## ISHTAR

In this book, I refer to Ishtar a great deal, and I have found her a useful "container" or "label" for many convergent ideas.

Ishtar was the most important female deity for the ancient Mesopotamians, who lived in the area that we now call Iraq. They called her the Queen of Heaven. Brooklyn Museum describes well the multifaceted nature of Ishtar: "She is the goddess of love and sexuality, and thus, fertility; she is responsible for all life, but she is never a Mother goddess. As the goddess of war, she is often shown winged and bearing arms. Her third aspect is celestial; she is the planet Venus, the morning and evening star."

In short, Ishtar's concerns are sexual pleasure, fertility, love, beauty, war and justice – areas of concern that our subconscious struggles with even today. Many of the messages we receive through our dreams come from these struggles. Our subconscious expresses its concerns to our consciousness via complex nervous system processes beyond our full scientific understanding. The platform for these messages is our dreams, and I use Ishtar as a label to give a name to the messenger.

The work the Mesopotamians did in the study of dreams, astronomy, astrology, mathematics, physics and the role of dreams in our lives has laid the groundwork for an extraordinary body of insight, knowledge and cultural norms we now take for granted. I use this body of work as a vessels of source material, and I use Ishtar to reference this encyclopaedic wisdom.

Ishtar, for me, represents the innate, intuitive wisdom we all possess – that brings messages from our sleeping, unconscious mind into our conscious awareness, and which the Mesopotamians heeded, documented and worshipped so devoutly. In this book, for the sake of transparency, clarity, brevity and poetry, I refer to this intuition as Ishtar and see her as our "dream goddess".

# About the Moon

In the previous chapter, we discussed the idea that our predecessors must have been "on to something" when attaching value to the metaphysics of the heavens and the predictive qualities of our dreams. While I have singled out the Mesopotamians as particularly visionary in pioneering these studies, many – perhaps even most – civilizations throughout history have invested in and relied upon some form of belief in the moon's energy.

I can't think of a single civilization or culture throughout history that hasn't considered the phases of the lunar cycle in its daily, monthly or annual decision-making. While it could be argued that the empirically minded are the exception, this sect is in its infancy, has brought nothing compelling to the table, and studies the moon relentlessly anyway. They even sent people there! So, let us not pander to any claims that the moon doesn't draw us in emotionally as surely as it does gravitationally.

Like it or not – whether you buy into it or not – for as long as humans have been humans, we have looked to the phases of the moon for some kind of inspiration. As much as we, a technologically advanced and scientifically driven culture, may have an itch to understand the physics that makes our species *feel* that the full moon does at least do *something* to at least *some* of us, the data is in and strongly suggests that it does affect us.

From Aborigines to Zulus, myths and legends are relentless in their assertion that the moon's phases have a terrestrial impact, whether this is physical, psychological, emotional, cultural, spiritual, artistic, religious, you name it. There is an overwhelming tide of testimony persuading me that even if we don't know the mathematical formula for its influence just yet, this doesn't dismiss the phenomenon as bunk. Humans don't *carve* the laws of the universe into being; we *realize* them – eventually. It's the height of conceit to think otherwise.

So, with that said, let us, with an open and curious mind, accept that there is something there. Let us review the historical interpretations of the phases of the moon and identify consensus, trends, tendencies and practices that deepen our appreciation of this breathtaking heavenly body and its influence upon the human psyche.

## THE EIGHT LUNAR PHASES

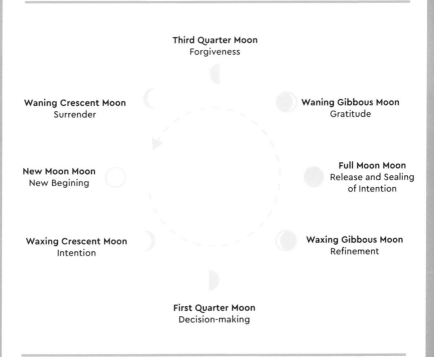

**Third Quarter Moon**
Forgiveness

**Waning Crescent Moon**
Surrender

**Waning Gibbous Moon**
Gratitude

**New Moon Moon**
New Begining

**Full Moon Moon**
Release and Sealing
of Intention

**Waxing Crescent Moon**
Intention

**Waxing Gibbous Moon**
Refinement

**First Quarter Moon**
Decision-making

The first thing we should look at is the anatomy of the lunar cycle.

While most of us are familiar with the new moon, the half moon and the full moon, these terms don't adequately describe the cycle to the degree we need. We actually need to identify and refer to eight distinct phases.

Here is a quick recap on the physics of the matter. We can see only the parts of the moon that are illuminated by the sun. Conversely, we can't differentiate between the blackness of the shadowed side of the moon and the blackness of the space behind it. As the moon orbits the earth, we see only the illuminated portions from various angles, with more of the moon's surface revealed to us when it is "behind" us and less when it is "in front".

This slow morphing of the visible portion of the moon throughout its orbit gives us this sequence of dark, waxing, full and waning lunar phases.

The historical consensus is that there is a need to identify eight discrete phases. (There are more, but we don't need to be that nuanced for this book.) Those phases are: the new moon, waxing crescent, first quarter, waxing gibbous, full moon, waning gibbous, third quarter and waning crescent. Each of these has unique qualities and interpretations.

## OUR INTUITION

Throughout history and around the globe, there has been a general cultural alignment of the significance of each lunar phase. Contrary to the opinions of our friends at NASA, the study of the moon isn't rocket science. What I find most interesting is that the more I learn, the more intuitive it all seems, and hopefully you will too.

For those of us who have paid even occasional attention to the cycles of the moon, either consciously or otherwise, we naturally end up keeping a kind of internal clock. In the same way that we can hazard a fair estimation of the time of day if we know it was noon about two hours ago; similarly, we unconsciously track the phases of the moon even if we only see the night sky periodically.

Most of us can appreciate intuitive relationships or analogies between the new moon and, say, the idea of fresh beginnings, the full moon and high energy, and the waxing and waning phases with emergent ideas and natural resolutions.

These two things – our internal lunar calendar, which innately knows the moon's phase, and our psychological relationship with that phase, which innately assigns emotional context – then mix with our unconscious thoughts.

And that is where the magic happens!

It is well documented that our dreams come from our primal subconscious and represent our fears, hopes, desires and, literally and figuratively, our dreams for the future. Add to the subconscious mix our awareness of the moon's phase and the psychological states we associate with them – whether this is of fresh beginnings, emergent ideas, resolution etc. – and it is a no-brainer; of course our dreams will be coloured accordingly.

In our sleep, our subconscious projects its fears and desires into our consciousness while the phase of the moon provides additional context. Combined, our dream and the lunar phase naturally offer more relevant data than either can offer on their own.

If we can become more familiar with the underlying psychology of our dreams and our relationship with the lunar phases, we will be more empowered to decode our subconscious projections and increasingly skilled at excavating deeper self-awareness.

What we do with this self-awareness is up to us, and we are certainly under no obligation to act. But those of us who have tried to interpret our dreams, or are curious about their significance, have an opportunity to delve deeper into the fascinating world of our revealed subconscious.

Before we get too ahead of ourselves, below is a guide to the phases of the moon and the consensus of their influence. These general principles can be used to frame our dream interpretations.

## THE NEW MOON

From day one of the lunar cycle and lasting for around three days, the new moon is a blank canvas on which all subsequent phases will be painted. It is a fresh start, a moment when we can be done with the past, file it away and start again. This is a moment of pure potential.

Likewise, our intuition and subconscious have an opportunity to neatly file "what was" and to consider the design of our future. This isn't a moment for action; this is a moment for pure creativity. A time to plant seeds, set intentions and identify, if only in our minds, what currently isn't happening but we wish will happen one day.

## WAXING CRESCENT MOON

From day four to day seven of the cycle, the waxing crescent is the thin curve of the moon that is visible just after sunset. Each subsequent evening, it will linger higher, for longer and illuminate more brightly.

A gorgeous artefact of the waxing crescent and its position relative to the earth and the sun is that, thanks to "earthshine" – the light reflected off the earth – the full circle of the moon is faintly visible against the blackness of the night sky.

The waxing crescent is analogous to the actioning of ideas with the prospect of their fruition etched as an outline yet to flower. It marks a time to plan and to see through to reality the opportunities we identified during the new moon. It is a time to make changes and shed more light on the things we desire.

The waxing crescent is a call to action.

## FIRST QUARTER MOON

From day 7 to day 10, and contrary to its name, the first quarter moon appears like a half circle. (The "quarter" refers to the moon's orbit, not the geometry of its visible portion.) It's neither new nor complete: it is split – neither one nor the other. It could be said that it has an identity crisis and may doubt its direction.

It is time to commit, and we can take inspiration from this moment to act accordingly. Following the waxing crescent and our planning for the future, the first quarter moon may be the first time that doubts or challenges present themselves.

Now is a moment when we can challenge ourselves to be aware of our surroundings and seek signs. If our waxing crescent plans are taking hold, many doors will open during the first quarter moon – doors of confidence and doors of doubt. It is time to steer the momentum. We must remember our intended destination and keep our eyes on the road.

Obstacles are good things; they are not meant to keep us apart from our desires; they are intended to keep everyone else out who doesn't want them as much as we do. We can use this moment to ask ourselves provocative questions, listen to our gut and act upon our answers.

We should re-engage with meaningful desires and *dis*-engage from meaningless whims.

## WAXING GIBBOUS MOON

Literally meaning "growing shape", the waxing gibbous begins around day 10 and stays until the full moon on day 14.

Growing in fullness, the waxing gibbous moon is ripe with potential. Increased light, size and imminent fulfilment conspire to emanate energy and tension that is at once potent and unresolved. We are not over the finish line yet, and it is time to close the deal.

Similarly, this phase of the moon communicates to us the most significant shift yet from the "potential energy" of the new moon to the "kinetic energy" of achievement. We can use this energy to inspire the sprint to the finish line. Good things are coming.

Yet this is no time for rushing the result. The devil is in the details, and this phase is all about focus, stamina and fine-tuning. Since we are in the waxing – building – phase, we should remain open to creativity and inspiration.

## FULL MOON

Arriving around 14 to 15 days after the new moon and lasting for three days, the full moon is the pinnacle or climax of the lunar cycle. It is a spectacle that doesn't age. I have been alive for nearly 600 full moons, and yet, still, on a clear night it takes my breath away.

Not even the most grizzled cynic can deny its splendour; such is the energy of this perfect circle of bright light and profound majesty that glides across its starry arc.

This moment of peak energy is powerful in many ways. Any peak is inevitably the start of decline, so there are opposing forces at play, and it is helpful to be aware of this tug of war.

Encouragement, relief and joy are all part of the pinnacle of the full moon, but it can also bring fatigue, feelings of anticlimax and frustration if things didn't work out the way we intended. Now is a good time to soften the ego and find peace with what is.

## WANING GIBBOUS MOON

Literally "declining shape", the waning gibbous moon begins on day 18 and lasts for three days. Receding from its peak, the moon rises later and later in the night sky and diminishes in size and brightness with each return. While there is a natural feeling of decline – of things no longer growing – this shouldn't be interpreted as negative.

If the new moon is the idea and the full moon is the party, the waning gibbous is the morning after. It is a time for tidying up, tweaking, weeding out the bad from the healthy, doing an audit and making some decisions.

Ask any gardener which is more critical: the seeding or the weeding? I think we innately know the answer – that these are equally important.

Now is a time for tidying up our spiritual landscape by cultivating, shifting, tweaking and planting seeds of change.

## THIRD QUARTER MOON

The third quarter moon begins at around day 21 and lasts for four days. It is both similar and a polar opposite to the first quarter moon.

It is similar because it is split in two, torn between the climactic energy of the full moon and the palate-cleansing new moon, and, as such, is conflicted and transitional. And it is opposite in that the illumination is a mirror image of its first quarter moon cousin.

Intuitively, this is again a time for choices. The focus of the third quarter is on clearing the way and inspiring catharsis. Quitting unhappy employment, toxic relationships or any other form of editing are all examples of actions manifested through the energy of cleansing. However, this should also be a time of reflection to avoid impulsive or reckless acts that may be detrimental to our best life.

In short, we should identify the adjustments needed and then make them. It is an awkward phase but one that can provide incredible insight, accountability and resolution; a time to bring balance to our lives.

## WANING CRESCENT MOON ☾

The final lunar phase, the waning crescent, occurs around day 25 and moves us out of the tension of the third quarter and into the blank slate of the new moon.

Just like the waxing crescent, the waning crescent is the thin arc that lights the edge of the faint circle of the dark side of the moon that is lit by "earthshine". If one phase of the moon is most underappreciated, it is the waning crescent. We are more likely to be asleep – literally and figuratively – as this waning moon rises just before dawn and we tend to overlook the opportunities for the insight it offers.

The waning crescent is a moment when we can see the past without being blinded by it. If we use this as a guide to fully clean our side of the street, heal or otherwise put to rest any persistent niggles, we won't rid ourselves of the underlying causes of our frustrations.

Psychologists call it closure. Others call it forgiveness, letting go or release.

I am the kind of person who likes to do the washing up just before I go to bed. That way, the kitchen will be clean when I wake up. This cleanliness sets me up for a happier day than if I were to wake up to last night's dinner still soaking in the sink. Just like washing or cleaning, this is how this phase relates to our lives.

The waning crescent encourages us to tie up loose ends before we end a chapter in preparation for the new day and the new moon.

# About Dreams

Some of my earliest recollections of my dreams are of flying, free from the constraints of gravity and earthly limitations. As children at the time, we all seemed fascinated with the wildness of our dreams and how they seemed to allow us supernatural abilities and insight.

As studied as I may be in the nature of dream interpretations, dreams still fill me with wonder. They are an endless source of inspiration and education in self-awareness, and no amount of study has dulled my interest in them or their power over us. Quite the contrary; the deeper I dig, the more there is to find.

Whether we are a seasoned scholar of ancient texts on dream interpretations or new to the idea that dreams hold more than simply comedy, there is always something new to learn about ourselves if we take a moment to consider what our subconscious has conjured up. It seems that science has the same fascination.

## WHAT THE SCIENCE SAYS

Freud and Jung were pioneers of the science of dreams. Both independently and in collaboration, they pushed back the boundaries of western psychology. They believed that dreams were directly connected with the psyche and the unconscious and deeply rooted in evolutionary biology. Both agreed that dreams are allies in healing mental illness. One interesting difference is that Freud looked back, tracing disease to repressed childhood trauma, whereas Jung looked forward, more interested in where dreams may lead us. Both neuroscientists published groundbreaking work in their field.

Other, more contemporary research has looked closely at evolution for inspiration. One such idea, known as "threat simulation theory", suggests that any species that can run simulations of threats in their sleep have a Darwinian advantage over species that have to learn "on the job". Another theory, the "activation-synthesis hypothesis", suggests that dreams are simply random images with no narrative meaning. It proposes that it is only upon waking that we humans try to superimpose meaning to the hotchpotch collage to which we were exposed.

In addition, I have read about REM, frontal lobes and delta, theta, alpha and beta brain waves. I have participated in sleep studies and consumed all I can find on the nature of dreams. But in the end, my personal experience suggests that the science of sleep talks more and more about less and less and is misdirected; it leaves me unsatisfied as if I were no closer to, and more distracted from, the truth.

Whereas my research into mysticism inspires me to dig deeper, my impression of the science is that it ends up sounding like mumbo jumbo and, to be honest, just sends me to sleep. Science has done little to scratch the itch I have in seeking meaning. I wish that were not the case, and I remain in hope.

## LIVING THE DREAM

Another interesting element of the popular dreamscape is the place that the word "dream" has in our culture: I am struck by how dumbed down and mundane the term has become. Expressions such as "living the dream", "hopes and dreams" and "follow your dreams" are trite social media memes that refer superficially to our desires for the future, yet have kept the idea in the mainstream only on a token level.

As widespread as the idea is that we must follow our dreams to be happy, it is remarkable how dismissive our culture can be when handed supporting evidence any more substantial and sophisticated than an Instagram post. Tell a friend arbitrarily that they must follow their dreams to be happy, and you will be met with near-universal approval. But suggest with good reason that dreams of aliens on the waxing crescent mean you should plant audacious seeds, and you may encounter more hostile responses.

I am aware that I may be introducing some "alternative" ideas in this book. It is healthy for me to keep in mind that these ideas can appear challenging and unorthodox for those not already immersed in what some may call "New Age" culture or mysticism. To address this, I have made all efforts to adopt the mindset of the sceptic and present these ideas in an unassuming way.

So, before I release the doves and embark upon the dictionary section of this book, I will take a moment to recap the roots, history, science, art and intuition of our dreams. I hope that this will reinforce the notion that there is much reason, thought, precedent and science that backs the ideas on which this book is grounded.

## THE FOUNTAIN OF YOU

Since childhood, we have known that our dreams represent our inner fears and desires. And since Freud and the advent of the sciences of the mind, there has been little debate from the academic world that our subconscious is a deep well of desire about which we know precious little but that which is projected through the mercurial prism of our dreams and unconscious behaviours.

Whole areas of psychology are dedicated to dream analysis to understand more about the fundamental nature of the dreamer. There is no debate that your dreams provide a constant, unedited, uncontrived, heartfelt stream of your inner life. Your dreams are the fountain of you, flowing straight from your subconscious and dancing in arcs throughout your mind, catching the light, sparking the imagination and informing the consciousness. If we can decode the messages, we can achieve a higher, deeper level of self-awareness than if we simply ignore them.

So, let's decode them.

Through incredible archeological work, we have been able to unearth, translate and interpret the wisdom of the Mesopotamian empire. Much of what we have found has forced us to rewrite history to show that this civilization's intellectual, mathematical and mystical advancements were millennia ahead of their time. Most tangibly, their mathematical prowess was inexplicably advanced, and, most interesting to me, their mysticism and explorations into astrology and dream interpretation were paradigm-altering. Using their goddess of dreams, Ishtar, as a figurehead, I have tapped this encyclopedia of the dream realm and refer to it in most of my work.

Then there is the great, silver goddess of the night sky – the moon.

Inextricably linked to the earth and inexhaustibly studied and worshipped in one way or another, there is no greater seductress of the human heart than the moon. Ever present, ever watchful and always spectacular, the moon's changing phases pull our emotional tides towards renewal, fulfillment, and waxing and waning evolutions in all we do, conscious or unconscious.

It is simply not possible for the average human throughout history not to have been intimately aware of the phase of the moon and to have their outlook at the very least subconsciously framed by the emotions evoked in the moon's shifting form.

# Whence the Moondust Lays

*Let no man say that the light of the Moon did not illuminate his way nor draw upon its sheen his hopes of yesterday.*

*Let no man deny that those who came before his time sowed for him fields of wisdom, whether or no he plucks of its bloom,*

*Let no man claim that the dark arts and the bright sciences are not woven as one, a tapestry of light, timeless and universal,*

*And let no man brag, proud and loud, that he holds all there is to hold, or that the doors to his enlightenment are closed even as he dreams of what might lie beyond their mind-forged locks.*

*Let our minds fly and dream, and hope and fear.*

*Let our hearts listen and learn and grow and perfect.*

*Let us walk this day with passion and purpose.*

*Let us sleep this night with creativity and openness.*

*And whence the Moondust lays, settled and still before the march of dawn,*

*Let us draw upon its silver sheen our hopes for the new day come.*

# Part Two

# The Lunar Dream Matrix

| Dream | New Moon ○ | Waxing Crescent ☽ | First Quarter ◑ | Waxing Gibbous ◒ |
|---|---|---|---|---|
| Aliens | Meditate on what you wish to manifest | Plant audacious seeds | Take a leap of faith | Meditate on how to perfect the art of your relationship with others |
| Alligators | Consider who and what might hurt you, and prepare accordingly | Be curious about others' activities without exposing your intentions | Act decisively | Strike first and fast |
| Babies | Do not hold back with your ambitions – you will grow | Unconditional devotion to new endeavours | Are you sure? | Tend to your life goals with love and kindness |
| Bears | Revisit old challenges as you are stronger now | Stand up and be counted | Finish the deal or take a time-out. Pick one | Trust your instincts – don't allow fear to have a vote |
| Being Chased | Take your self-care responsibilities more seriously | Start tidying up | Stop running | Look for opportunities to settle debts |
| Cars | Are there better ways to get there? | Pick a new destination and start packing | Upgrade your life vehicle before it breaks down | What life vehicles can you tinker with? |
| Cats | Acknowledge your deepest desires | Who is lurking like a cat in your life? | Is it time to pounce? | Be more aware of your surroundings |
| Current Partners | However you would advise your dream self about relationships is the advice your waking self needs to hear about your life | Learn from the mistakes your dream self makes | Use your dream emotions to inform your decisions | Ask for what you want. You might just receive it |
| Death | Don't hide your pain | Move on | Strike at the heart of antipathy lest it be the death of you | Cut the mooring rope if you wish to sail |
| Dogs | Plan your ideal garden of relationships | Pursue intriguing new relationships | Reflect on how you can "get out of your own way" with relationships | Seek ways to fine-tune and deepen well-established friendships |
| Ex-Partners | Don't call the ex-partner, recall the ex-feeling, and consider how to meet up with that | Superimpose desired feelings onto your current waking life. Manifest them | Play the game of love for the love of the game | Fine-tune new love with lessons learned |

| ● Full Moon | ◑ Waning Gibbous | ◔ Third Quarter | ☾ Waning Crescent |
|---|---|---|---|
| Accept the things you can't change | Confront negative elements in your life; they won't bite | Remove yourself from hurtful situations | Let go |
| Beware of still waters | Trust your instincts and take small, evasive actions | Now is a time for daring | Watching is more important than lashing out |
| Accept your situation and rise to the challenge | What are you prepared to sacrifice for the greater good? | Think hard about your next steps | Sign on the dotted line |
| Be strong, and fight for what you believe | Remove the arrow that wounded you | Hibernate | File challenges under E for Experience |
| Develop better ways to manage the things that cause stress | Develop contingencies, just in case | Confront your concern and be done with it | Resolve to resolve the issue |
| Adopt a better attitude toward the obstacles in your way | Fix the problem | Denying emotions will only bring more upset | What can you do to secure your relationships? |
| Use your femininity | Take care of yourself, and have fun | Reject your runts | Lay down your arms and curl up by the fire |
| To everything, there is a season | Forgive, but don't forget | Make healthy decisions at the end of play | Honour your past decisions, even if they didn't turn out as you had hoped |
| Give the seeds of your success water and time. | Release the dead weight in your life | Burn down the old to make space for the new | Few things last forever. Be grateful for the moments you had |
| Accept the limits of challenging relationships, and don't take the challenges personally | If you could prune your circle of friendship, consider where you might trim | Distance yourself from toxicity | Seek to heal through dialogue, forgiveness or simply letting go |
| Your heart is a flower | Let your leaves fall with grace | In love, your gut instinct is right | Accept loss not as failure but as nourishment |

| Dream | ○ New Moon | ☽ Waxing Crescent | ☽ First Quarter | ◐ Waxing Gibbous | |
|---|---|---|---|---|---|
| Falling | Get out of your own way | Attend all your life's planning sessions | It's never too late to say, "This is my stop" | Don't forget to put a bow on it | |
| Fish | Know what you wish to catch before you bait your hook | Dive into the ocean of your desires | Reel in opportunities | When you trawl for opportunities, be sure your net is fit to catch them | |
| Flying | From what do you wish to take flight? | Remove the things that prevent you from feeling uplifted | Pay for your ticket to freedom | Keep your spiritual GPS switched on | |
| Guns | Lay down your arms and retain your power | Remain flexible in the roles you play in life | Choose to choose | Are you aiming at the right things in life? | |
| Hair | Mirror, mirror, on the wall, are you being fair to yourself? | Express emotions without acting out on them | Nurture traits that better suit your ideal self-image | Detangling life knots will add bounce to your stride and shine to your smile | |
| Hotels | Consider your next move with special care | Keep in touch with your personal anchors | Have a plan in your back pocket for what's next | Tend to the details of the transient elements of your life | |
| Houses | Renovate your life | Make some psychological home improvements | Don't dither at the threshold of opportunity | Spruce up your internal décor | |
| Money | Follow your heart, find your bliss | Invest in your spiritual wellbeing | Place your emotional bets | Balance your spiritual budget | |
| Nakedness | Know your strengths and play to them | Remove masks of pretense | Allow yourself to be more authentic | Dress for success | |
| Poop | Fight clean from this point forward | Treachery abounds | Open up | Clear the air | |
| Pregnancy | Imagine without limits | Take small steps toward your goals | Choose to unlock mind-forged manacles | Labour can be hard so remember to breathe | |

| ● Full Moon | ◗ Waning Gibbous | ◖ Third Quarter | ☾ Waning Crescent |
|---|---|---|---|
| Focus not on the outcome of your endeavours but on the effort you put into them | The more frequently you attend to your emotional balance, the less dramatic any adjustments need to be | When you close doors softly, others will open effortlessly | Don't go to bed angry |
| Don't release the good in the hope of netting the perfect | Be tenacious, but don't be obsessive | Choose achievable goals over wishful thinking | Optimism will always attract more of what you require than pessimism |
| Enjoy the view | Take responsibility for how grounded you are | Expect turbulence, but don't let that stop you | Breathe in the new, exhale the old |
| Don't ask, "Can I?" Ask, "*Will* I?" | Identify your fields of freedom | Focus on what you see, not what you fear | There is more power in flexibility than in flexing |
| Make the most of what you have | Trimming off the split ends of life will improve your spiritual condition | Cut off life's tangles. You will look better | Tend to your inner beauty as diligently as you tend to your outer beauty |
| Enjoy your stay | Leave your home when you debug it | It's time to depart from dependency | Wherever you go, know where home is |
| Allow your garden to grow as you, and only you, wish it to | Maintain a good spiritual housekeeping routine | Dump emotional clutter | Secure the healthy things in your life |
| Cash in or settle up | Are you in exchange? | Spend less time on unfulfilling activities | Submit your spiritual tax return |
| Let your true characteristics shine | Where are you exposed to harm? | Beware of wolves in sheep's clothing | Button up |
| Life is messy. Accept it rather than wallow | Pull up weeds when you see them | Flush negativity | Tidy up with integrity |
| Peace of mind is the most important ingredient in the formula for success | Confidence is as easy as Plan-ABC | Keep your life goals out of harm's way | Nurture your creations with love and patience |

| Dream | ⬤ New Moon | ☽ Waxing Crescent | ◗ First Quarter | ◑ Waxing Gibbous |
|---|---|---|---|---|
| **Sex** | Consider your choices in life | Pursue your best self | Commit to your chosen path | Enlighten up and work toward your bliss |
| **Sharks** | Never stop fighting for what you want in life | In a world of fish, be a shark | Facing your fears is the only way to make them go away | Maintain your emotional toolkit |
| **Snakes** | What can you do to live more authentically? | Be honest in matters of the heart | Don't accept no for an answer | Prepare for the worst so that you can expect the best |
| **Spiders** | Where are you stuck? | Tread carefully | Choose silk relationships | Turn up to collect your reward |
| **Teeth** | Consider where in life you desire more control | Set achievable goals to reclaim your voice | Ask why you let others make decisions for you | You are about to blossom |
| **Time** | Prepare | Be kind to yourself in your planning | Consider your bigger dilemmas, weigh the pros and cons, and move in a healthy direction | Do away with the devil of stress by letting go of its hold on you |
| **Tornadoes** | What if you could wipe the slate clean? | Risk ruffling feathers if you wish to fly | Remain objective and proceed with courage | Ask others for support |
| **Water** | Your life will only flourish where you water it | Breach the sands of inertia and allow life to flow | Act with decisive energy when the right wave comes your way | Be mindful of the gardens of love you nurture |

| ◐ Full Moon | ◓ Waning Gibbous | ◗ Third Quarter | ☾ Waning Crescent |
|---|---|---|---|
| Manage your relationship expectations | Seek ways to recharge existing bonds | What is hindering your growth? | Seek to heal old emotional wounds |
| Most of your concerns are statistically harmless | If you smell blood, get out of the water | Are you as kind as you would like to think? | Stop thrashing, and you will know the way |
| Be still, reflect, and have faith | Look out for red flags regarding trust and loyalty | Stick to the path | Lie supine, rest, and rejuvinate |
| Go about your business with tenacity and patience | Rebuild and shine on, despite the setbacks | Don't neglect the quiet corners of your life | Practice gratitude, and send out positive vibrations |
| Express your character with joy and confidence | Delegate | It's time to detox | Nurture others |
| Make time for your own standards, and don't waste time worrying about the opinion of others | Good, fast, cheap; pick two | Reassess your assumptions to see if they are still relevant | Resolve the unresolved in a positive way |
| It's what you do in the eye of the storm that will set you apart from others | Batten down the hatches | Seek shelter | Separating the things that soothe us from the things that chafe |
| Seek spiritual balance and reflect that in everything you do | Carry an umbrella in case it rains | Planning will ground us, while indecision will wash us away | Find an emotional safe harbour until the skies clear |

# Part Three

# Dream Interpretations

# Aliens

When we look up into the night sky, we seek what we know. Be it the phase of the moon, the North Star, Cassiopeia or Betelgeuse, it is comforting to seek the familiar within the unfamiliar. Because, in all the range of experiences we humans share as a species, there is nothing more terrifyingly lonely and diminishing than to gaze into the void of space and try to comprehend its vast emptiness. Human minds evolved to navigate the terrestrial, not the extra-terrestrial, and we are simply not equipped with the capacity, tools, intellect or technology to get our heads around it.

The extra-terrestrial represents all things beyond our understanding. Dreams of aliens are visitations from Ishtar, pointing out that there may be dimensions to the universe, our world, our lives and our everyday awareness that we have yet to connect with. Some things may be alien to us now, but we may still learn from them in the future.

There is a poetic symmetry to our alien dream when we compare its timing to the lunar month. All dreams are coloured by the phase of the moon during which they occur, and alien dreams are no different. With both the subject and timing of these dreams inspired by the universe – which informs our subconscious of our future desires – one can't fail to feel we are all threads in the infinite fabric of the universe, in all its dimensions.

In fact, alien dreams go deeper than that.

As I have mentioned in the earlier parts of this book, the Sumerians and the authors of the Clay Tablets of Babylon were so advanced that some have speculated that the origins of their intellect must have been inspired by something beyond the terrestrial. Their civilization doesn't make linear sense when plotted against the rest of humanity. It would be irresponsible not to question such a profound spike in the otherwise smooth arc of human development. The Sumerians, Egyptians and Incas have opened up the conversation about alien intervention in human affairs through their art, engineering, mysticism and dream interpretation. If these discussions are not entertained, at least in a small part, in books such as this one, then where should we discuss them?

Dreams of aliens have ample metaphors. They also have their literal interpretations. Ideas of parallel dimensions, the origin of human DNA (and life in general, for that matter), intelligence and radical thinking, and the relentless pursuit of meaning all have plausible explanations when we consider that our planet is not the only one in the universe that contains life. As soon as we open ourselves to the possibility that we are not alone, all bets are off.

Whether our dream contains metaphorical or literal meaning, we should be sensitive to more subtle details of alien dreams. Was the dream a visitation? How did we feel in their presence? Did we feel fear? In what way do we feel alienated? In what way do we alienate others? In what way or with whom are we seeking to connect?

## Dreams of Aliens on a New Moon

**KEY THOUGHT:** Meditate on what you wish to manifest

The new moon is a time of re-invention. We can't gaze at the first razor-thin sliver of light as the moon begins its slow illumination and not wonder what the future holds for us. Often, it can be challenging to tap into our inner self to ask what we desire.

With dreams of aliens, Ishtar is telling you to try to separate – alienate – yourself and spend time alone to meditate on your desires.

Your social life may be rich, pleasurable and meaningful but it is irrelevant, or, worse, detrimental, if you are not centred. Meditation, silence, "me-time", yoga, walks and even journal writing are excellent ways to remove yourself and focus on what's really important to you.

## Dreams of Aliens on a Waxing Crescent Moon

**KEY THOUGHT:** Plant audacious seeds

Dreams on the waxing crescent moon represent a sign for you to begin to action ideas and turn your wishes into reality. It is a time to plant seeds. Through dreams of aliens, Ishtar wants you to know that you should act on some things that seem outside of your circle of influence, ability or perhaps your awareness.

This can be a challenging time. How can you initiate ideas that are outside your circle of awareness? The short answer is: you can't. The more inspiring message you can glean from this dream is that you may be aware of this idea yet have somehow dismissed it. You may think of it as outside the circle of possibility, overambitious or more than you are worthy of. Whether it is a well-paying job, a gorgeous date or an ambitious fitness goal, consider this dream a nudge from Ishtar to go for it anyway.

Daffodils and oak trees both come from humble beginnings. Dreams of aliens on the waxing crescent moon are a message from Ishtar that you shouldn't let the audacity of the desired result scare you from planting its seeds.

## Dreams of Aliens on a First Quarter Moon

**KEY THOUGHT:** Take a leap of faith

The quarter moon is neither new nor complete. It is undecided and lacks commitment. More importantly, when commitment is required, a lack of action is a commitment in itself to give away your power. Put another way, if you don't decide, someone else will. This makes alien dreams during this lunar phase particularly exciting.

There are things in life you know, and there are things you don't know. All that you don't know – all that is alien to your awareness – is up for grabs in the dream you have experienced and the message it contains. Now is an exciting moment when you must take a leap of faith.

Quit work and start a freelance career. Put a deposit down on a holiday to a location you know nothing about. Buy that property on a hunch. File for divorce when you know it is the right thing despite the fear of not knowing how you will get through it.

Or don't do any of this, and be at peace with the fact that you are giving away your power through inaction.

Alien dreams on the first quarter moon are an encouragement to take a leap of faith and trust that the universe will take care of you.

## Dreams of Aliens on a Waxing Gibbous Moon

**KEY THOUGHT:** Meditate on how to perfect the art of your relationship with others

The waxing gibbous moon inspires you to take what you have committed to and fine-tune this for completion. With most of the graft behind you, knowing when to stop can often be a unique challenge. Indeed, many renowned artists believe that art is not what you put in; it is what you leave out and to know when to stop adding.

Finessing your life projects – family, relationships, work, self-image – requires confidence of vision, and 100 per cent confidence can elude most people most of the time.

Alien dreams represent Ishtar's message that you must explore the unknown for answers. How often do great ideas pop into your mind while you are on a long walk or in meditation? You may not know the origins of your ideas, but Ishtar does, and she knows that you can tap into higher dimensions when you silence the noise of you everyday life.

Take a moment to take a time out. Take a walk and tap into that meditative state that allows new thoughts to reveal themselves. Reflect on ongoing challenges – of family, relationships, work or self-image – and see what the universe advises on how to complete your work of art.

## Dreams of Aliens on a Full Moon

**KEY THOUGHT:** Accept the things you can't change

Dreams on the full moon tell us that Ishtar wants you to recognize completeness. This could relate to relationships, endeavours or any other journey you have embarked upon. Only you can know the relevance to your life. Dreams of aliens present a recognition that you are estranged from something and that Ishtar wants you to bridge that gap.

The alien dream on the full moon is a powerful moment to seek acceptance of things that are out of your control. It is time to find peace in the knowledge that you are who you are – warts and all – and to stop putting fruitless efforts into believing otherwise.

If you can accept the things you can't change, you are well on the road to serenity.

## Dreams of Aliens on a Waning Gibbous Moon

**KEY THOUGHT:** Confront negative elements in your life; they won't bite

Dreams on the waning gibbous moon are typically a sign from Ishtar that you have an opportunity to trim the fat and edit out some of the mildly negative elements in your life. Dreams of aliens – alienation, the unknown – can provide critical pointers on how to go about this pruning and, indeed, what to trim.

Two avenues can be taken as a healthy response to this dream; remove the unknown from the issue or remove yourself to reflect.

In removing the unknown from the issue, you can seek to confront the problem head-on. Often, you can resolve a misunderstanding in challenging or strained relationships by simply seeking better communication. Try to engage, as it takes courage to confront problems. The fascinating thing is that facing the problem is usually a lot less painful than you feared. These are called paper tigers; things that appear intimidating but are paper-thin and harmless.

In removing yourself to reflect, you can seek silence and meditation and give yourself the space to identify these paper tigers.

## Dreams of Aliens on a Third Quarter Moon

**KEY THOUGHT:** Remove yourself from hurtful situations

The third quarter moon is a defining moment showing what is what will no longer be. Unlike the first quarter moon, which asks you to make commitments *toward* a goal, the third quarter seeks your commitment to letting go; acceptance.

Dreams of aliens should make you aware of the alienation you have felt or caused. So, dreams of aliens in the third quarter moon suggest that strong emotional messages of acceptance are being sent to you.

You can use this as inspiration to ask yourself if you have caused pain or alienation or have suffered these hurts through the actions of another. Then you can decide what you want to do with this awareness.

Deciding to reconnect with old friends or end a problematic relationship are the kinds of actions you shouldn't only consider, but initiate if you want to. Ishtar is telling you that now is the time to amputate the wounded limb, whatever it may be, and she knows you will be healthier for the action you take.

## Dreams of Aliens on a Waning Crescent Moon

**KEY THOUGHT:** Let go

The waning crescent is the moon's closing thought: its swansong. These are always kind thoughts. Dreams of aliens on the waning crescent moon are messages from Ishtar that there are some things that you may never fully know and that fretting over them will cause unnecessary anguish.

Questioning why a partner left you, or why an unfortunate or even tragic event happened to you or someone you know, is completely valid while you seek psychological closure. Yet there will come a time when dwelling on a past event becomes less healthy and eventually unhealthy. The dream of aliens on the waning crescent moon is a reminder that your subconscious seeks to resolve any lingering thoughts and you have done everything you could. Ishtar knows it is time to let go.

# Alligators and Crocodiles

While alligators and crocodiles have many fearful attributes, including strength and sharp teeth, perhaps their most potent psychological weapon is their stealth. Hidden in water that may be a swamp or an idyllic lagoon, they lurk almost entirely concealed, approach in silence and strike with lightning speed.

This combination of near invisibility while hunting and shocking speed in attack strikes fear into those that witness it. While you may never consider swimming in a swamp, the thought of alligators would put anyone off trusting even the most picturesque of tropical lagoons. This is the symbolism that becomes attached to your subconscious: trust.

Alligators destroy trust and ruin the reputations of the most innocent situations if there is a hint or rumour of their menace. They sow deceit and doubt, and while the chances of an unsuspecting soul who chooses to stand by the water's edge coming to harm are slim, on the wrong day an alligator's merciless attack will be so swift it is essentially inescapable.

Dreams of alligators carry much the same message: deception, mistrust, power, danger, unexpected attacks and a cold lack of emotion.

In fact, "crocodile tears" – the water released from the reptiles' eyes as they attack that appear to be a cruel and insincere display of fake emotion – has become a catchphrase for fake, manipulative emotional displays in humans.

Tragically, this real-life emotional fear has excused some unnecessary commercial gain, with alligator and crocodile skin becoming a trophy material for luxury goods. This prize hasn't escaped the awareness of our subconscious, with their hides representing opportunity.

Alligators and crocodiles have a poor public image but some redeeming qualities. Dating back to the age of the dinosaurs, and relatively unchanged since, they know a thing or two about survival and are supremely well designed. They are an evolutionary success story, even if this is one you don't want to be a part of in reality.

That said, meeting alligators or crocodiles in your dream is a different story that can provide insight and wisdom.

## Dreams of Alligators and Crocodiles on a New Moon

**KEY THOUGHT:** Consider who and what might hurt you, and prepare accordingly

Dark, mysterious and filled with unknowns, water and the new moon have much in common. We can only wonder what lurks beneath the surface of unfamiliar waters, behind the eyes of our family and friends, or beyond the relative predictability of the near future.

Dreams of alligators or crocodiles on the new moon are a message from Ishtar that you must do more than "only wonder" what lies beneath, behind and beyond what you know. This dream is a call to imagine what opportunities and threats may catch you off guard.

The way to illuminate the metaphorical murky water is to ask, "What is the worst that could happen?" This simple question filters the murk into clarity. If you can imagine what may hurt your intentions, half the battle is won.

Dreams of alligators on the new moon are messages for you to consider who and what may hurt you and prepare accordingly.

## Dreams of Alligators and Crocodiles on a Waxing Crescent Moon

KEY THOUGHT: Be curious about others' activities without exposing your intentions

As an alligator or crocodile seeks its desires, it glides gracefully and silently through the water with only its eyes and perhaps the top of its back and its head breaking the surface. But that is all it needs to be able to see and then approach its prey.

The waxing crescent moon is similar in that you see only a hint of its form gliding across the early evening sky, chasing the setting sun. Dreams of alligators on the waxing crescent tell a story of the pursuit of goals while revealing little to your opponents. Depending on the specifics of your dream, this alignment of parallel narratives – the crescent of light on an otherwise suspicious moon and the suspicious gaze of a predator in otherwise still waters – could suggest that you should keep your cards close to your chest as you plan future endeavours or be wary of others who may be concealing their own hand. That is to say: you are hiding something from others, or others are hiding something from you.

If you believe the former is the correct interpretation, be careful with whom you share your plans, in case they betray you and spoil the opportunity. If the latter feels more applicable, watch for predatory eyes plotting something that may hurt you.

Either way, it is in your best interests to be curious about others' activities without exposing your own intentions.

## Dreams of Alligators and Crocodiles on a First Quarter Moon

**KEY THOUGHT:** Act decisively

A thirsty antelope stands by a watering hole that it suspects may be the hiding place of an alligator. Should it risk drinking?

Sometimes in life, you may be met with dilemmas that force unpleasant choices. To drink would risk an attack, and to abstain risks dehydration. When you are faced with these unknowns, the should-I-shouldn't-I can drive you crazy.

The dream of alligators on the first quarter moon is a transitional time as the light struggles to dominate the shadow and as you struggle to make your choices. The alligator can snap quickly, and you can also dip in and out quickly.

So, with dilemmas, you can either struggle with indecision or go with your gut, act decisively and move on, accepting that acting decisively, generally, gets you what you desire, even if sometimes you fall prey to hidden dangers.

# Dreams of Alligators and Crocodiles on a Waxing Gibbous Moon

**KEY THOUGHT:** Strike first and fast

Dreams of alligators on the waxing gibbous predict opportunities in your life that you should see through to completion. The waxing gibbous moon is generously illuminated but still holds secrets, shadows and doubts. For the moon, fulfillment is only a matter of time, but for Ishtar, it is a matter of details – things that must be completed.

The alligator is a primed and primal killing machine when submerged, yet it must emerge to strike. But when it is trapped, it becomes meat for other predators or luxury items for human opportunists. It is a sad and grim reality, but there is an undeniable association between the overpowering of this menacing animal and the social value of the spoils.

Dreams of alligators on the waxing gibbous moon are Ishtar's way of telling you there are gains to be had, but you must strike first – and fast – to grab the opportunity.

# Dreams of Alligators and Crocodiles on a Full Moon

**KEY THOUGHT:** Beware of still waters

Unlike alligators that strike fast and surprise their prey, there is nothing quick or surprising about the full moon. We have watched it wax to completeness, and here it is. Yet what can be surprising, or at least anticlimactic, is whenever anything is fulfilled, completed or whole, how disappointed we may feel compared with the anticipation of the moment.

The full moon reveals the whole picture in full illumination. You must be prepared for the light it sheds and the picture it reveals.

Dreams of alligators on the full moon reveal a picture of danger, deceit, concealment and predatory behaviour. This dream is Ishtar's warning that menace is in your midst and you must beware, especially of still waters.

## Dreams of Alligators and Crocodiles on a Waning Gibbous Moon

**KEY THOUGHT:** Trust your instincts and take small, evasive actions

As the moon moves into its waning phase, it is time to start consolidating your gains and prepare for the coming shadow. Doubts begin to creep across the lunar surface, and new concerns should be kept at bay.

With dreams of alligators or crocodiles on the waning crescent moon, you see that these new concerns are subtle but ominous. All it takes is the sight of two eyes peering out from just beneath the surface of the water to let you know that they represent far more danger than you can see.

Ishtar is telling you that if you don't take action, these dangers will grow in importance and strike at any time.

By trusting your instincts and taking small evasive actions in the short term – such as excusing yourself from a social obligation that you don't feel comfortable about or declining an opportunity that seems too good to be true – you can likely save yourself greater harm in the long run.

## Dreams of Alligators and Crocodiles on a Third Quarter Moon

**KEY THOUGHT:** Now is a time for daring

While it is apt to protect yourself from the alligator or crocodile in your dream, it can also be worth considering the scenario from the reptile's perspective, or, more helpfully, considering yourself to be the reptile.

Dreams of alligators or crocodiles on the third quarter moon are clear signals from Ishtar that the shadows are looming, and if you wish to reach your desired goals, you must lunge out of the murky waters of indecision, doubt or fear and go for the kill.

The alligator knows that lunging out of the water exposes itself to vulnerability. But if it doesn't lunge, what's the point? It is the same with you and your goals: you must lunge. Now isn't a time for caution. Now is a time for daring, commitment and trust in your preparation. You should act soon before shadows hide the way.

## Dreams of Alligators and Crocodiles on a Waning Crescent Moon

**KEY THOUGHT:** Watching is more important than lashing out

Just as an alligator hides in dark waters, peering stealthily above the surface, so does the waning crescent moon. During this phase, the moon reveals its light as just a sliver against shadow. You can interpret this as a guide to be the alligator in your dream.

Dreams of alligators during the waning crescent tell you that while the majority is lost, over or happening without you, now isn't the time for you to strike or be overt and active in pursuing your desires.

While the "money shot" in nature programmes shows an alligator going for the kill, 99 per cent of the work of any successful endeavour you undertake involves watching, learning and gathering information. Watching is more important than lashing out, as that is when you discover most about the vulnerabilities of your opponents.

# Babies

Throughout this book, I discuss innate instincts that humans have evolved. The spirituality and psychology of our developing species are complex. What isn't complex is the fact that none of it would be possible without our instinct to protect our children. If this weren't a primal function, we would have died off long ago. Cherishing and protecting our children, especially when they are babies and at their most vulnerable, is an evolutionary necessity and at the heart of our existence.

In our dreams, babies represent many positive things; all that is precious to us, new starts and rebirth, fresh ideas, optimism, innocence, purity and our "inner child". They can also project primal fears. Anyone who has lost a child, even for a few minutes in a public space, will know that there is no panic like not knowing where our children are.

It is no surprise then that dreams of babies are some of the most common and powerful we can experience. What the baby does in the dream can dramatically alter the interpretation of the dream, and the sub-categories of baby dreams could fill a book by themselves. Pre-natal (before birth), being born, crying, playing, needing to be changed, giggling; these all have different meanings.

Here we will concentrate mainly on the timing of the baby dream, and I encourage you to reflect on its behaviour in the dream and seek meaning within the interpretations based on the lunar cycle.

There is much historical and indigenous belief that the full moon affects a woman's menstrual cycle, triggers labour and is associated with rebirth. (Indeed, the word "menstrual" is derived from the Greek word *mene*, meaning moon.) Contemporary studies suggest the jury is still out on this one, although it is widely accepted that modern artificial lighting and modern lifestyles have disrupted such synchronicity. Regardless, belief that the moon and birth are interconnected has been consistent across time, cultures and continents.

## Dreams of Babies on a New Moon

**KEY THOUGHT:** Do not hold back with your ambitions – you will grow

Dreams of babies signify that there is new life, new hope and new responsibilities on your forecast. This is a creative dream that promises much yet isn't without burden. It is possible that you may need to mature a little to manage whatever is in store for you. But don't worry, the rewards will be worth it.

Dreams of babies on the new moon are particularly creative. The new moon is pure potential without light defining its form. During this lunar phase, you have the opportunity to think about fresh starts, endeavours, relationships or desires. This dream is Ishtar's way of telling you not to hold back on your ambitions.

Great things are in store for you, but you can't achieve them if you don't first aspire to them. The baby in the dream informs you that you may need to fill bigger shoes. This dream is telling you to have faith in the process and in yourself. Through it, Ishtar is assuring you that, though you may not feel ready now, you will mature and rise to the occasion, and the rewards will be worth it.

## Dreams of Babies on a Waxing Crescent Moon

**KEY THOUGHT:** Unconditional devotion to new endeavours

Dreams of babies on the waxing crescent moon signify that ideas bubbling away inside you are starting to form, and you now need care and attention to bring these endeavours to the surface.

Ishtar is doubling down on this message. The waxing crescent is the nascent moon calling you to act on your passions, and the baby in the dream represents something precious that you must nurture with devotion.

Take a moment to review everything in your life that feels new, and take inspiration from the baby in the dream to focus serious attention on getting it right. You may be embarking on a relationship, a career move, a creative project or even self-care. Whatever it is requires your full attention.

You should also note the baby's behaviour in your dream; giggling, crying, hungry, sleeping, etc. Visualize what that behaviour means to you, think about the appropriate response to the baby's needs in your dream, and project that response onto your waking life endeavour. This means you are doing Ishtar's work.

## Dreams of Babies on a First Quarter Moon

**KEY THOUGHT:** Are you sure?

Raising a child is a huge commitment, and is a responsibility not to be taken lightly. A baby requires devotion, emotional maturity and physical stamina. It is not for everyone, and the timing has to be right. Dreams of babies challenge you to ask yourself if you are ready.

Dreams on the first quarter moon represent a transition from shadow to light, with equal parts illuminated and hidden. Dreams during this lunar phase call on you to make difficult decisions, and the baby in your dream is Ishtar's caution that you must be prepared for what is coming.

Whatever it is in life that promises a new start – a new relationship, a career move, a house purchase – will undoubtedly be a dramatic shift. This shift may be more than you are ready for. Is the timing right?

Dreams of babies on the first quarter caution you to think hard about the work and responsibility required if you are to take your next big step in life. The timing has to be right, and if it isn't right, it isn't too late to take a step back and ask if you are sure this is the right thing for you.

## Dreams of Babies on a Waxing Gibbous Moon

**KEY THOUGHT:** Tend to your life goals with love and kindness

The devil is in the details, and beauty is in the little things. Dreams of babies on the waxing gibbous moon are clear signs that you are gathering power to succeed and that attention to detail is required to perfect the vision you are nurturing.

The waxing gibbous moon is almost ripe, with only a sliver of shadow remaining. These shadows represent your remaining doubts – and doubters; they are diminishing but still nag. Attention to detail will seal the deal.

The baby in your dream represents your precious possessions, attributes, traits or endeavours. Think about what the baby is doing in your dream and recognize your emotional response to it to decide the best way to move forward with your life goals. If the baby was crying, did you want to comfort it? Maybe your investors, partners or collabourators need some reassurance. If the baby was sleeping, were you happy to leave it alone? If so, you should have faith that all is well and not change your course. If the baby needed changing or feeding how did you care for it? Think about how you can tend to your life goals to keep moving forward.

Tend to your life goals with love and kindness.

## Dreams of Babies on a Full Moon

**KEY THOUGHT:** Accept your situation and rise to the challenge

Dreams of babies on the full moon are rich with meaning and energy. The dream signifies that you have been delivered a gift in life, although it may be a challenge and may test your maturity. The baby in the dream is a precious gift that requires your care, emotional stability, patience and devotion; in return, it will deepen your life experience.

Take a moment to ask yourself what the baby represents. This could be a new job, a new relationship status or a new mindset. What is challenging you to grow?

The timing of the dream is significant in that it should prompt you to see that this situation won't change any time soon. The die has been cast. If you've been unsure about whether your circumstances will change, fade or evolve, you can glean from the full moon that it is now your responsibility to accept your situation and rise to a higher calling to meet the responsibilities gifted to you.

You may not be ready yet – you may need to "grow up" – and if that's the case, so be it.

## Dreams of Babies on a Waning Gibbous Moon

**KEY THOUGHT:** What are you prepared
to sacrifice for the greater good?

Life can be a challenge, and it can be incredibly rewarding. You can't always avoid pain, but you can avoid suffering depending on your attitude toward challenges. Dreams of babies on the waning gibbous moon represent new opportunities to redefine who you are and ask what you are prepared to sacrifice to achieve a greater goal. If you can accept the sacrifice as an investment in something bigger, you can be more at peace with it and mitigate any "suffering".

For example, it is easy to say you want more money, but are you prepared to get a second job to earn that, if you can? If so, great. However, if you're not prepared to sacrifice your evenings and weekends, then maybe you don't want money more than you want your evenings and weekends. Likewise, you may want to be fitter, but are you prepared to go to the gym at 6 a.m. on four days every week or exercise every day?

In short, gain doesn't come without a price tag.

Ishtar doesn't judge you – she is only asking.

Dreams of babies on a waning gibbous moon represent your desire for self-improvement and ask what you are prepared to sacrifice for the greater cause. Once you determine what you are prepared to give up (time, money, friendships, comfort, etc.), you should maintain a good attitude about what you gave up, knowing it's the right decision.

# Dreams of Babies on a Third Quarter Moon

**KEY THOUGHT:** Think hard about your next steps

Dreams on the third quarter moon represent a time to make decisions. This is a time of transitioning from light to shadow, yet neither is dominant, and there is tension between dark and light. Dreams of babies represent precious endeavours in your life that require time and energy.

Ishtar is pointing out that you need to make some big decisions. There may be life-changing shifts in your future – in the real world or in your creative thinking – that will require sacrifice if you proceed. The waning moon demands commitment, and it is up to you to consider the light and the shadow – the pros and cons – and act with clarity.

You can find guidance by examining the baby's behaviour in your dream. Is it crying, happy, hungry, sleeping, needy? If you look inward when considering its demeanour, you may become aware of your emotional response to the baby. It is essential to recognize this emotion as it is a predictor of your emotions in the waking world if you are to proceed. If your emotions were positive in the dream, the pros win. If your emotions were negative, you should think hard about your next steps.

# Dreams of Babies on a Waning Crescent Moon

**KEY THOUGHT:** Sign on the dotted line

Dreams of babies on the waning crescent moon are exciting because they predict meaningful new energy in your life that need "signing off".

When we think of the most significant commitments we make in life – perhaps who we marry or buying a property – while the commitment is large, the actions are subtle. "With this ring, I thee wed" and "sign on the dotted line" are both small acts that signify huge life commitments. Telling someone we love them is another.

As the moon prepares to close out its cycle and disappear into shadow, you must clear up any uncertainties about your commitments to the most significant treasures in your life.

# Bears

The human emotional relationship with bears is complex, often contradictory and counterintuitive. Anyone who has come face to face with a bear will know these are powerful and intimidating creatures. Yet they also retreat, hibernate and lead reclusive, solitary lives. Who didn't have a cuddly bear as a child? So, are bears to be feared, do they fear us or are they a spirit of comfort?

They are all those things, and dreams of bears are fascinating for that reason.

Humans' long relationship with bears appears to be more intuitive and spiritual than cultural. This bond is well documented in Mesopotamian, Assyrian and Arabic history, with bear imagery on cave walls and clay vases revealing their posture and power. Even the night sky honours the great bear, and the animal has always represented protection, hope, death and power.

Generally speaking, bear dreams contain positive messages even if the bear is hostile. When interpreting bear dreams, it is often helpful to regard the bear as a symbol of rivalry, requiring you to defend your position.

Dreams of a hostile bear represent a rival trying to supersede you. If you kill a bear, you will overcome an opponent, or you will experience loss, and a bear skin represents strength and courage.

You can also examine the type of bear you encounter. Polar bears, for example, numb themselves to endure the cold, and this has clear analogies with cold emotions – yours or your partner's – and the need for warmth and healing.

Lastly, hibernating bears communicate that there is value in retreating – spending time alone – to rediscover yourself, your strength or your purpose.

## Dreams of Bears on a New Moon

**KEY THOUGHT:** Revisit old challenges as you are stronger now

The new moon is an exciting time to redesign your future. This lunar phase gives you the opportunity to consider all possibilities and select with a clear mind your ambition for the coming weeks and months.

Dreams of bears on the new moon represent a call to arms. The bear in your dream is a rivalry that has revealed itself. While this rivalry may seem to be challenging you, this is not Ishtar's intent. She is letting you know that you are ready to consider upping your game and taking on new challenges.

Take a moment to be purely creative. Adopt the courage of a bear and assume you have the courage to move forward with any goal. Consider all aspects of your life where you have challenges, especially those that you have long felt were lost.

It is said in circus lore that to train a strong animal, you tie its leash to a stake in the ground. As a baby, the animal won't have the strength to pull the stake out. And by the time it's strong enough, it will have given up hope that it is possible to pull itself loose.

Have you given up on any challenges in your life? Perhaps you are now strong enough to confront them. Ishtar thinks you are ready.

## Dreams of Bears on a Waxing Crescent Moon

**KEY THOUGHT:** Stand up and be counted

Waxing crescent dreams are exciting beginnings. Now is the time to stop thinking and start acting. This is when change really starts to occur.

Bear dreams on a waxing crescent can represent challenging and exciting transitions. Since the bear represents rivalry or opposition in some form in your life, the dream is Ishtar's way of saying that it is time to push back on areas of your life that have frustrated you.

Whether this is a professional relationship, a personal one or even an individual goal like health or weight, whatever form the rivalry takes, now is your calling to take steps in defence of your mission.

Stop wishing. Start pushing back against the things that are thwarting your goals. The steps you take don't need to be impressive, conclusive or decisive; they just need to be a step in the right direction. As the saying goes, a journey of 1,000 miles begins with a single step.

Now is the time to stand up and be counted.

And the exciting thing is that when you look back at all you have achieved, you will realize that this first step was when the tide turned in your favour.

## Dreams of Bears on a First Quarter Moon

**KEY THOUGHT:** Finish the deal or take a time out. Pick one

When the moon is in its first quarter, it presents you with indecision. Are you in or out? The position of the moon represents competition and hibernation. Now isn't the time to make big, rash decisions. If you have been experiencing some challenging times, this dream is a sign that you should consider stepping back and taking a break.

If you take an audit of your life profile, you should try to identify areas of rivalry or conflict that cause extended frustration. Ishtar is calling on you to consider your next moves carefully. Usually, your options can be boiled down to two choices: yes or no – forward or backward. The bear dream is undoubtedly a sign that a challenge you are facing needs commitment one way or another.

A bear's options are to fight or hibernate, and this provides a nice analogy when assessing your next moves in situations that challenge you. Hibernation doesn't represent failure; it offers you a chance for emotional regrouping, self-care, rest, nourishment and reflection. If you feel fatigued, take a moment to recognize that you can't run on empty, and note in your calendar when you will take up the cause again. This isn't defeat; it is care.

Or, you may decide that you are in the home stretch of a challenge, and now is a good time to rally your energy and get it done.

The point is to commit to one or the other. Indecision is the wrong decision. Any conscious decision is the right one.

## Dreams of Bears on a Waxing Gibbous Moon

**KEY THOUGHT:** Trust your instincts – don't allow fear to have a vote

Dreams on the waxing gibbous moon represent the growing form of the visions of yourself and your life. The moon – your desire – is close to being fully formed and now needs only final touches.

Dreams of bears on the waxing gibbous moon communicate that challenges, rivalries or other projects that have demanded your full effort are coming to a close. Now they need that final push. The waxing gibbous moon reveals what was hidden. You should do the same; reveal hidden passions and follow your gut instinct. You should trust in your strengths and abilities.

As with most things in life, nothing that is worthwhile comes without effort. And not everything you do will be met with universal approval. You may have to fight for your goals, and that is okay. You may or may not win those fights, but one thing is for sure – you won't win if you don't try. It is often right at the end of an endeavour that you can let your guard, and yourself, down.

In "Aesop's Bear and the Two Travellers" fable, the two travellers are surprised by a bear in the woods. Out of fear, one traveller abandons his companion. The moral is that it is not at all wise to keep company with someone who would desert a friend in a moment of danger. If you consider the two travellers to be two sides of your psyche, you can see that the side operating from a place of fear isn't good company for you; it will abandon your better self.

You should trust your instincts and not allow fear to have a vote.

## Dreams of Bears on a Full Moon

**KEY THOUGHT:** Be strong, and fight for what you believe

Just as bears represent emotional rivalry, the full moon represents the pinnacle of that emotion. Dreaming of bears on a full moon may come at a time of exhaustion, frustration or even anger. However, the dream shouldn't increase any feelings of frustration. Instead, it should bring relief.

The bear dream on a full moon is about good and bad times, a cycle that you can't control. It is a time of forces governing your fate and the turning of the tide. Whatever tug of war you have been locked in may have taken its toll. The good news is that it has peaked, and Ishtar knows it.

It is time to soften. Take a breath. Put the rope down and release that tension. You have given it your all, and now take some time alone and meditate on your challenges. And remember: when a bear is threatened, it becomes protective and ready to fight for what it believes is right.

In life, you win some, and you lose some. But you will lose some more if you don't take time to reflect on what it is you fight for and what you learn from your interactions with others. This can only be achieved through reflection and meditation. Then, be strong, and fight for what you believe.

## Dreams of Bears on a Waning Gibbous Moon

**KEY THOUGHT:** Remove the arrow that wounded you

The waxing gibbous moon is the beginning of its diminishing light and shape, which speaks to you about your desire for resolution.

Dreams of bears in the waxing gibbous moon provide you a perfect time to consider the conflicts and rivalries with which you may struggle and think about which ones are worth pursuing and which are simply an unnecessary drain of your energy.

There is a Buddhist story of a man shot by an arrow who spends his energy asking why, how and who – wanting to understand the injustice – while neglecting to remove the arrow from his body.

Sometimes, walking away from a draining rivalry is a net gain. Through this dream at this time, Ishtar is prompting you to consider pruning the conflicts in your lives and pulling out the arrow that wounds you. A bear wouldn't indulge feelings of injustice; it would deal with what wounded it.

## Dreams of Bears on a Third Quarter Moon

**KEY THOUGHT:** Hibernate

The third quarter moon asks you to commit. Unlike the first quarter moon, when Ishtar asks you to commit to letting things in, during the third quarter she asks you to commit to letting things go.

Bear dreams represent rivalries in your life, positive or negative. Either way, they can be exhausting. Bears hibernate when they are at the end of their season, and you can learn from the way they know when it is time to retreat.

Take this moment to recognize that your energy is finite and that you must be selective with how you expend it.

Take time out. Hibernate. Find some time to reflect on how best to budget your emotional reserves so you can nourish your body and soul.

If this means removing yourself from toxic situations, fantastic.

## Dreams of Bears on a Waning Crescent Moon

**KEY THOUGHT:** File challenges under E for Experience

The Asian black bear is recognized for its small size and a waning crescent moon shape on its belly. It is known locally as the "moon bear" and is regarded as a good luck charm. Dreaming of bears on the waning crescent represents good luck and an excellent opportunity to reflect.

The waning crescent is a time to tie loose ends so that they can be stored properly. Bear dreams represent challenges, rivalries or conflicts in any part of your life. When you dream of bears during this phase of the lunar cycle, these two ideas coincide to present a powerful alignment that can bring much-needed peace.

There is nothing wrong with a friendly rivalry, and there is little to gain from unnecessary or toxic rivalry. Bear dreams represent both, so you shouldn't be quick to assume all conflict is negative. Yet there comes a time when a rivalry is trying or obsessive and if left unchecked this will become unhealthy.

Take a moment to ask yourself if you are finished playing the game. Give credit where credit is due. Be grateful that life is so interesting and can teach you so much. Recognize that it isn't the winning or losing that is important; it is the learning.

If you learn from your interactions and file them all under E for Experience, you always win.

# Being Chased

Sometimes, life may feel like a rollercoaster, while at other times it may feel more like a merry-go-round. One has emotional ups and downs, and the other is more mundane. But note that they both go round in circles; they start, progress on their trajectory and return to their starting place. And so it is with life: we are created from the universe, cycle through days, months and years on our life trajectory until we finally return to the universe that created us.

On these cycles, we will experience light and dark, and our task is often to avoid the darkness and pursue the light.

This idea of pursuit isn't a mere analogy: throughout history, humans have chased and been chased for sport and for survival. We pursue relationships, careers and life goals. Sometimes we even become so fixated on the "thrill of the chase" that we lose sight of the goal: the chase becomes the goal.

In all cases, the chase symbolizes trying to avoid consequences. This can come with its own consequence: anxiety. We have all heard stories of fugitives eventually handing themselves in after years on the run, when their anxiety finally caught up with them.

While we would like to think of ourselves as independent, this is far from reality for most of us. We rely on many others, and many others rely on us. We all have responsibilities to ourselves and others, and we expect these responsibilities to be met. Civilization is virtually defined by this expectation. When obligations are met, the world functions as we would want. However, when obligations aren't met – fairly or not – someone somewhere is usually to be held responsible for the perceived injustice. And that is the essence of the chase dream: holding to account.

The stress of everyday living puts an incredible burden on our psyche, and we can't assume that everyone we know has voiced precisely what it is they expect from us. Let's be fair – we are unlikely to have clearly expressed that either. And again, this applies to the responsibilities we have to ourselves. We all know when we procrastinate, and no one else will chase us up on such private things except Ishtar.

A few interesting factors in "being chased" dreams are helpful to be aware of, such as the identity of the pursuer (known or unknown, employer, family), the nature of the pursuer (human, police, animal, monster, killer, etc.), the distance between them and you, and your ability or inability to move with ease. Identifying these factors can help you zero in on the meaning of this dream for you.

## Dreams of Being Chased on a New Moon

**KEY THOUGHT:** Take your self-care responsibilities more seriously

The new moon is a time of pure possibility, new beginnings and fresh ideas. This is a time for planning and "dreaming" of what you want and forming a vision of your future self. It is an exciting time.

Yet it is also a time of shadow: a form yet to emerge.

Dreams of being chased represent some form of avoidance of responsibility – something that has been causing you frustration. The root cause may be something real or something only Ishtar knows. Regardless, this dream tells you there is something you are consciously or unconsciously avoiding that should be addressed.

Avoidance of responsibility for something already in place seems to contradict the new moon's potential for creating positive change, but this is the exciting part of this dream. The new moon is all about new possibilities.

It is entirely possible that what you are "avoiding" is your responsibility to yourself to live your best life. The question from a dream of being chased on a new moon is: How can you run from the shadows in life without fully understanding the form that is yet to emerge?

It is time to start thinking about what you have always wanted, and acknowledge your responsibility to care for yourself. Allow your desires to take form, whether this is to do with your health, a better grip on finances, writing that book you know is in you, or taking that painting course you could never justify. Now is the time to take your self-care responsibilities more seriously.

## Dreams of Being Chased on a Waxing Crescent Moon

**KEY THOUGHT:** Start tidying up

Dreams on the waxing crescent moon are Ishtar's way of saying that it is time for you to initiate projects, actions and fresh endeavours. With this dream of being chased, she is also letting you know that some responsibilities you may have been avoiding aren't going away and should be addressed.

The waxing crescent is when the moon begins to illuminate. Now is an excellent time to take an audit of everything that has been nagging at you. Just as the moon moves from dark to light, you should examine what is in your shadows. Whether reviewing the household budget, joining the gym, paying off a credit card or apologizing to a loved one, consider what action you could take today that would lighten your burden.

We are sometimes advised to keep our side of the street clean; in other words, to take care of our responsibilities before blaming others for not taking care of theirs. This is a nice turn of phrase. Yet often, we can't clean it entirely in one go or may not even be fully aware of the things that need cleaning.

But you can make a start. If you can identify one action that would begin the process, this dream asks you to make that move.

## Dreams of Being Chased on a First Quarter Moon

**KEY THOUGHT:** Stop running

Dreams on the first quarter moon represent a time of choice; decisions are needed in some area or aspect of your life. Remember, the first quarter moon is half in light, half in shadow. It is difficult to see the whole picture, and Ishtar is asking you to think about the shadows in your life. This is a time to control the narrative of your journey: dark or light, left or right, should you or shouldn't you?

This is a fascinating time to experience a dream of being chased. This category of psychic messaging relates to removing the shadows of worry and responsibility, or, more precisely, concern regarding avoiding responsibility.

When you are being chased, you have options: to continue your avoidance or turn and face the music. Few worries actually prove to be true. Most often, when you turn to face your fears, they turn out to only be something fearful in appearance but lacking in substance.

Ishtar can't promise that the issue pursuing you will be a paper tiger. She is, however, assuring you that it would be in your best interest to either turn and confront the nagging issue or simply stop worrying about it.

Either way, stop running.

· · · · · · · · · · · · · · · · · · · · · ◗ · · · · · · · · · · · · · · · · · · ·

## Dreams of Being Chased on a Waxing Gibbous Moon

· · · · · · · · · · · · · · · · · · · · · · · · · · · · · · · · · · · · · · · · · ·

**KEY THOUGHT:** Look for opportunities to settle debts

· · · · · · · · · · · · · · · · · · · · · · · · · · · · · · · · · · · · · · · · · ·

The waxing gibbous moon is when the light of the moon is almost full, and the messages you divine from this phase of the lunar cycle relate to details in the completion of psychic endeavours.

Dreams of being chased during the waxing gibbous moon are complex, often depending on the pursuer in the dream and your emotions while being chased. The good news is that the timing of the dream means that you have the opportunity to perfect your situation if you attend to the finishing details.

The waxing gibbous is an emergent phase, transitioning from dark to light. It isn't complete, and similarly, maybe there hasn't been enough energy, money, time or love in waking life, and you have been trying to escape this reality. Ishtar is urging you to see that there is more to come.

Perspective is key, and the waxing gibbous encourages not just a "glass half full" attitude but a "glass getting filled".

Is the chase changing your positive perspective in life? If the chaser was frightening, it could suggest your anxieties are affecting your perception. If the pursuer is related to finance, are they far away or right behind you, as you may need to look at your budget and fine-tune it. If you are laughing in the dream, enjoying "playing hard to get", if you like; look at what you can do to clinch the deal to your satisfaction, knowing that your pursuer wants what you have.

You are almost out of the woods. Look for opportunities to settle debts.

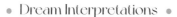

## Dreams of Being Chased on a Full Moon

**KEY THOUGHT:** Develop better ways to manage
the things that cause stress

The full moon is a time of high energy, fulfilled missions and, sometimes, unmet expectations. It can be both a climax and an anti-climax. Either way, this is a turning point and denotes a shift in energy from action to resolve. This is a special time when most light is cast over the moon, naturally urging you to use its energy to uncover your current anxieties.

When you are being chased in your dreams, the pursuer represents the worry experienced by your psyche. After a chase dream, it is important to try to identify the pursuer as this can often help you to identify what is worrying you, and this is when it gets interesting and challenging.

At the full moon, Ishtar is telling you that, like it or not, the issue isn't going away. This fact can challenge your ego or maturity. Challenges like these can be very tricky to accept, sometimes painful to address, but are always much needed – and Ishtar knows this.

Whatever the nature of the pursuit, it is time to accept that this is a fact of life. Debt, work, responsibilities to others, limited time, etc., are things you would be better off accepting and addressing in an adult, systematic way rather than avoiding. It is time to develop better ways to manage the things that cause you stress.

## Dreams of Being Chased on a Waning Gibbous Moon

**KEY THOUGHT:** Develop contingencies, just in case

The waxing gibbous moon presents the gift of closure. During this moon phase, shadow is beginning to encroach on what was previously illuminated. It urges you to accept your worries. If you don't find complete closure, then at least you have the opportunity to start to tidy up messy situations in your lives.

What better time to experience a dream of being chased. Because this category of dream represents a form of chronic psychic stress, this is certainly a burden you would be better off without.

Even dreams in which you seem to be enjoying the chase may not be entirely positive during the waxing gibbous moon. Things will eventually catch up with you in one way or another, and you want to ensure you are in a good place when that happens.

Now is a time to tweak your actions such that if and when your worries do catch up with you, you are ready. You would be well advised to consider worst-case scenarios and have contingencies.

## Dreams of Being Chased on a Third Quarter Moon

**KEY THOUGHT:** Confront your concern and be done with it

The third quarter moon is a dynamic moment that dovetails remarkably well with the category of dreams that involve being chased.

The specific relevance of the dream requires some understanding of your pursuer, so take a moment to identify the psychic reason for the pursuit (work, family, health, etc.). Ishtar is advising that you are avoiding something, and the timing of this dream shows that she is urging you to commit one way or another to the matter at hand.

The third quarter moon is in decline, at its midpoint between light and dark, and seeks a commitment to resolution: closure. It seeks a decision.

If you can identify the source of the concern that prompted the dream of being chased, use its timing as a prompt to turn and face your pursuer. Confront your concern and be done with it.

## Dreams of Being Chased on a Waning Crescent Moon

**KEY THOUGHT:** Resolve to resolve the issue

The Babylonians knew that the waning crescent was the closing of a chapter and started a new calendar month during this phase of the lunar cycle. This is intuitively the completion of the cycle, and time to resolve issues and finish tasks.

When you are being chased in your dream, this can represent any number of different worries. Clues in the dream can help you zero in on the real-life issue at hand. The pursuer, how close they are, your attitude in the dream, and your ability to move (or not) are all pointers that can help you analyse the message you are being given. Once you have an idea of the meaning of the chase, you can think about your attitude toward the issue.

The timing of the dream, the waning crescent moon, prompts you to wrap things up. It is better to avoid having things spill over into the next lunar cycle. Even if you can't resolve the issue at hand quite so quickly, you can at least decide to resolve the issue.

After all, Ishtar isn't concerned about the actual issue; she is only concerned that you are worried about it and wants you to be free from the burden of indecision.

# Cars

Where would we be without cars? Stuck at home, most likely. Ever since the Mesopotamians invented the wheel in 3,500 BCE, cars have literally and metaphorically been the vehicles we use on our journey to our desired destination. While car dreams are rarely literal, we use so many car metaphors in everyday life that the language for cars and the interpretation of car dreams are virtually interchangeable.

Do you feel you are in the driver's seat in life, or do you feel like a passenger on life's journey? Has your career stalled, or does it need a jump start? Are you living life in the fast lane? Are you on the right track or lack direction? Do you need to shift gears? Do you ever feel you need to apply the brakes? Has your relationship broken down? Do you need to refuel? And the list goes on. So, identifying surface-level interpretations of car dreams may as well be literal.

There are deeper layers, too.

How you feel in the dream is essential. Are you excited or anxious if you are speeding in the dream? The condition of the car is also relevant. Flat tyres may mean you could benefit from patching up old friendships? Overheating could suggest stress, missing parts may imply reaching out to new business colleagues, and rust could indicate limited time.

Generally, these dreams are all about holding onto control. However, car crashes represent feelings of losing control or worrying about making an error. If you have allowed someone else to sit in the driver's seat, this represents a feeling of having given power or control away, having handed over the keys to your successor.

How much you rely on a car in your waking life will determine your dream's symbolism. The details of the dream communicate how you are coping with your life's journey, and the timing of the dream provides additional context.

## Dreams of Cars on a New Moon

**KEY THOUGHT:** Are there better ways to get there?

Dreams of cars on the new moon present a fascinating prompt to examine your current "vehicles" in life and ask if they still suit your needs.

The new moon is a time for infinite possibilities cloaked in shadow. It is your responsibility to examine what these shadows are hiding and see if you can find new ideas. The car represents the things in your life currently moving you along, such as your job, marriage or friends.

Other important things to note are the car's condition and your role in the dream. These refer to your role in the decision-making and the quality of the vehicle.

Ishtar has a message, but it is for you to decode. You must compare the quality of the journey in your dream to that in your waking life and then ask yourself, are there better ways to get there?

## Dreams of Cars on a Waxing Crescent Moon

**KEY THOUGHT:** Pick a new destination and start packing

Dreams of cars on the waxing crescent moon are bold statements from Ishtar that you need to take a close look at the profile of your life, identify areas on your "ambition map" that are mostly in shadow yet still call to you, and find ways to get there.

For most of us, when we were younger, we could list many things we wished to do. As time goes by, for good practical reasons, we start to limit that list. But we don't need to be so black and white about it. We can still dream. And we do. In fact, that is what dreams are for.

This dream is a prompt from Ishtar to pull out that list, add to it, pick a new destination and start packing.

## Dreams of Cars on a First Quarter Moon

**KEY THOUGHT:** Upgrade your life vehicle before it breaks down

The quarter moon is a dynamic time in the lunar cycle. Half illuminated and half in shadow, we know only half the story and must uncover the rest. We must base decisions on knowing we can't see the complete picture. And when the facts aren't clear, we must go with our gut.

Dreams of cars relate to the "vehicles" you use on your life's journey, such as friends, work, interests, lovers, etc. Just like cars, these life vehicles rarely last forever. No one wants to trade in a car that works perfectly well, so they tend to hang on to it until it breaks down one too many times.

It is the same with life vehicles.

Wouldn't it be better to trade in your vehicles before they break down? A healthy vehicle is a beautiful thing. If that vehicle is showing signs of age, or you don't feel happy driving it anymore, consider revamping it.

In dreams of cars on the first quarter moon, Ishtar is showing you in vivid ways how you feel and how your vehicle is performing. If there are red flags, think hard about trading it in.

## Dreams of Cars on a Waxing Gibbous Moon

**KEY THOUGHT:** What life vehicles can you tinker with?

Dreams of cars on the waxing gibbous moon are a clear sign that you have opportunities to improve the route you are taking in life via the vehicles you are using to move forward.

You need to relate the emotional, logistical and mechanical conditions of your dream experience to your waking life journey and identify what Ishtar may be saying to you. How are your work opportunities that keep you moving financially, your relationships that keep you engaged emotionally, and the interests that keep you stimulated intellectually?

If you meditate on these dream factors, it usually becomes clear what Ishtar is referring to. Unless the dream is of you in the driver's seat excitedly cruising in the fast lane in a brand new automatic car (suggesting everything is great, don't change a thing), you can usually find a "problem" within the dream (and in your waking life) that could be tinkered with.

When you hear a rattling sound in your real car, you need to lift the hood and take a look, or, better, take it in for a service, and you can do the same in all areas of life. Further education for work, a vacation or some honest conversations with your partner, a yoga retreat for spiritual care, or retail therapy for a closet update are all ways to service your vehicle.

## Dreams of Cars on a Full Moon

**KEY THOUGHT:** Adopt a better attitude toward
the obstacles in your way

How many times have you heard that life is a journey, that it isn't about the destination but is about the "getting there". This is true. Arriving at a physical location you have always wanted to visit can be an anticlimax when the anticipation was so much more engaging.

Dreams of cars on the full moon carry messages to enjoy the journey.

Firstly, the moon lights your way in full brightness. It doesn't get any brighter – any better – than this. And secondly, the car in your dream may not be perfect (or maybe it is), but it is taking you anyway, even if it is slow, has a flat, needs refuelling or is rusty.

The dream may appear to be about the obstacles preventing you from getting to your destination. But Ishtar is being ironic. The message isn't about the destination; it is about the journey. Adopting a joyful attitude toward the obstacles in life that prevent you from reaching your destination will improve the emotional quality of your journey.

## Dreams of Cars on a Waning Gibbous Moon

**KEY THOUGHT:** Fix the problem

As the moon enters its waning phase, its light begins to fade, and some of its surface returns to shadow. This is a time to see what isn't working and call it a day.

With dreams of cars during this lunar phase, it is important to recognize a few things. Firstly, the car is a metaphor for the control you have in life and the power you have to get where you need to. Secondly, your emotions in the dream and the condition of the car tell you what is or isn't working.

Are you a passenger in life, letting others do the steering? Is there traffic where too many other people are competing for what you want? Is the car overheating, stressed and requiring a cooling-off period? Are you going too fast or too slow? In this dream, Ishtar is presenting the way she thinks you can fix some of the problems in your life so you can feel more empowered.

But her advice isn't worth the parking ticket it is written on unless you fix the problem.

## Dreams of Cars on a Third Quarter Moon

**KEY THOUGHT:** Denying emotions will only bring more upset

Dreams of cars on the third quarter moon are all about releasing emotions. These tell you that things that relate to your life journey need to be reconciled emotionally.

Just as the car represents the vehicles you use in life, the third quarter tells you that some elements are illuminated – working – and some are in shadow – not working. Washing a car may make it look better, but if it doesn't perform well or makes you unhappy, life is too short to accept this as the only option, and you shouldn't settle for superficial fixes.

You must take note of the emotions you experienced in the dream, as these are the truth. Whatever you feel in the dream, you feel in life, except you may be better in waking life at repressing or justifying these feelings. This is a good short-term strategy, perhaps, but a terrible long-term one.

If it is time to trade in the job, the friend or lover, denying that emotion will only bring more upset.

## Dreams of Cars on a Waning Crescent Moon

**KEY THOUGHT:** What can you do to secure your relationships?

As the moon enters its waning crescent phase, it becomes almost entirely hidden in shadow so you can see very little of it.

Dreams of cars during this phase tell you that there may be tweaks to the things you do in life that could improve and secure your control over your life journey. You must fix the little left that is visible.

If you can identify what the car represents – a job, an interest, a partner, a self-image, etc. – and connect with the emotion you experienced in the dream and the condition of the vehicle, you should be able to see opportunities or positions of control.

The last thing you do to a car at the end of the day is park it and lock it up, as these small actions make sure it will still be there for you tomorrow. After dreams of cars on the waning crescent moon, you can ask yourself what you can do to care for your relationships to ensure they are maintained.

# Cats

From classic witches and black cats to the cat lady down the street, there is a well-earned stereotype that cats and females have a deep connection. Elegance, affection, fighting to protect, sensitivity, nurturing, a love of rest and luxury are all feminine and feline traits. Cats and females share darker characteristics too. Secret, stealthy, domestic yet untameable, free-spirited, cunning and, well, "catty" women and cats have historically been linked in many ways.

Let me clarify: I believe we all have masculine and feminine traits. Some men exhibit more feminine traits and, likewise, some women exhibit more masculine characteristics. While the stereotype is the cat lady, the witch or the Egyptian goddess – all females – dreams of cats refer to the feminine in all of us.

As with all dreams, its subject is just one component of the message. Its behaviour in the dream tells you more. How you relate to the cat in your dream can provide useful information, too. A happy cat communicates bliss. An aggressive cat suggests feminine hostility in an area of your waking life. A biting or scratching cat suggests someone untrustworthy that you should be cautious of, and so on.

Cats are crepuscular – my favourite word. This means they operate at twilight and hunt in the shadows, seeking what is hidden. Dreams of cats can often be a prompt for you to do the same. If you have ever tried to catch a cat that doesn't want to be caught, how did that work out?

The term "herding cats" refers to a difficult or impossible task; likewise, dreams of chasing cats suggest you may have challenges ahead.

And, of course, beyond the subject and its behaviour, the timing of the cat dream will provide further insight.

## Dreams of Cats on a New Moon

**KEY THOUGHT:** Acknowledge your deepest desires

Cats on the new moon tend to be more relaxed. Of all the dreams and lunar cycles in this book, I think few are more seductive and intriguing than dreams of cats on the new moon.

The full moon is a time shrouded in shadow and mystery. It begs for you to look for things that are hidden. The moon itself is hidden, and it casts no light. You are blind to its help. Yet how often is it that, when asked to imagine something new, you close your eyes to shut out distraction? Only then can you conjure creative visions from the deep recesses of your mind. Often it is in the dark that your imagination is at its wildest.

What do cats do in the dark? They hunt. They pursue their desires, even if they can't yet see them.

Dreams of cats on the new moon are a potent sign to acknowledge your deepest desires, even if you currently have no idea how to achieve them.

# Dreams of Cats on a Waxing Crescent Moon

**KEY THOUGHT:** Who is lurking like a cat in your life?

With the waxing crescent moon now appearing in the dusk skies, it begins to work its magic, and its work to achieve fulfillment has begun. This is a time when your subconscious tells you that things in your lives require similar initial efforts in your goals to achieve fulfillment.

Starting 7,500 years ago, Mesopotamian farmers domesticated wild cats to combat mice infestations. Cats were symbolic of Mesopotamian life and often seen as an omen of the will of God. This gateway in your dream is Ishtar asking you to think about who the cat in the dream represents in your waking life.

Assuming the cat in the dream wasn't you, it represents a person in your life – most likely a female or a situation led by a female – that is challenging you. You need to consider who or what the cat represents in your life. Who is lurking like a cat or has cat-like characteristics?

If you can identify what the cat represents in your waking life, you are halfway there. You will be required to take action, but you can't be sure what, precisely, Ishtar is cautioning you about until you examine the behaviour of the cat in your dream. Was the cat sleeping, scratching, biting, hunting, grooming or attacking?

Your next challenge is to relate to how you felt in the dream toward the cat. If you felt empathy and it was hungry, you should nourish it. If it was cozy, you can be content. If it was aggressive, you should look deeper into what is bothering you in your waking life. Alternatively, if you had no feeling for the cat or felt disdain, you may want to remove a problem from your life.

How you treat the cat is the message Ishtar is sending you – what you need to do in your waking life. But first, you must determine who the cat is.

## Dreams of Cats on a First Quarter Moon

**KEY THOUGHT:** Is it time to pounce?

Dreams of cats on the first quarter moon represent a time to commit. The moon is half in shadow and half illuminated. It sees what it wants to be but is in doubt.

When cats hunt, they prowl, stalk and eventually pounce. Often when they stalk, they twitch as they consider the exact moment to pounce. This should-I-shouldn't-I is what the cat on the first quarter moon is all about: when to pounce.

This book can't advise on what it is that you should (or shouldn't) pounce on. But you will know what it is. If this is unclear, pay attention to the cat's behaviour for clues to the identity of the waking-life concern.

Dreams of cats of the first quarter moon are Ishtar's way of saying this is the time to commit. It is time to pounce.

## Dreams of Cats on a Waxing Gibbous Moon

**KEY THOUGHT:** Be more aware of your surroundings

Most often, dreams are signals from Ishtar that she has concerns, like a suggestions box. Rarely do people suggest we keep things just the way they are. Suggestions are about minor tweaks to improve a component of our lives, and dreams on the waxing gibbous moon are suggestions for completing the picture.

Like cats in the night, this dream urges you to be more aware of what is around you, your environment, people and your career, and to evaluate where you are now so that you can proceed with confidence.

Dreams of cats represent the light and dark sides of femininity. It is critical that you understand not just the behaviour of the cat in your dream but also your feelings toward it if you are to link it to your waking life and glean meaning and inspiration.

If you take a moment to consider the female interactions you have and the challenges you may face with each of these, you should be able to identify who Ishtar is referring to.

Back to the suggestions box. How did you manage the cat in the dream? Did you stroke it and provide comfort and reassurance? Did you feed it? Did you retreat from its hostility? Whatever it was that you did, this is what Ishtar is suggesting you apply to your current challenges in your waking life.

## Dreams of Cats on a Full Moon

**KEY THOUGHT:** Use your femininity

Cat dreams on the full moon are a potent combination of the power of fulfillment and the power of female instincts. Energy on the full moon is heightened. Studies have found that cats are more active during the full moon, and this could be because there is more light. You may feel more reflective than usual; more open to intuition.

Cat dreams on a full moon communicate a time of endings, female energy and femininity – grace, gentleness, sensitivity, beauty and maternal instincts. The timing of the dream is no coincidence. The moon is at its most brilliant; full, complete and perfectly illuminated. It lights the night sky more brightly and for longer than any other time in its cycle. It shines a light on what would otherwise be obscured in shadow.

The dream indicates you must sit with your thoughts to project your grace, gentleness, sensitivity and maternal instincts. These are strengths; use them.

## Dreams of Cats on a Waning Gibbous Moon

KEY THOUGHT: Take care of yourself, and have fun

As the moon begins to wane, the energy of the night sky retreats in time, light and shape. This is a time to start winding down and worrying less about the outside world. Cats are generally more playful during a waning gibbous moon, and you should be too.

Dreams of cats on the waning gibbous moon pertain to your playfulness and femininity and how you use this in your daily waking life. While some of a cat's activities include hunting, stalking and prowling, it spends more time grooming, resting, playing, purring and sleeping. Having a playful spirit means being easygoing, free and joyful. You are fully involved in what you do rather than thinking about your daily responsibilities.

When you look at the things you desire and the work you put into achieving them, don't forget that the cat paces itself and knows how to take care of itself. It knows there will be a time for hunting, and that time will be more rewarding if it is content and energized.

Take care of yourself. Have fun.

## Dreams of Cats on a Third Quarter Moon

KEY THOUGHT: Reject your runts

Dreams on the third quarter moon are messages from Ishtar that you need to make decisions, sometimes tough ones. The new moon is approaching, and you must solidify your position.

Dreams of cats represent your feminine side. One significant feminine trait is your maternal instinct: your desire to nurture and protect. Female cats have the same maternal instinct with one exception; if there is a runt in the litter, the mother may reject it. While this sounds cruel, this is a tough but practical decision to reserve the milk for the kittens most likely to survive. Caring for the runt may not save it and may jeopardize the greater health of the litter.

Likewise, if you can identify your "runts" – the low-quality, unhealthy elements in your life that divert energy from more worthy endeavours – and reject them, then you can up your game and improve the overall health of your brood.

## Dreams of Cats on a Waning Crescent Moon

**KEY THOUGHT:** Lay down your arms and curl up by the fire

There comes a time in every cat's hunting expedition when it returns home, regardless of its "success", and curls up to sleep. Hunting isn't purely a means to an end; it is a lifestyle, an innate process. Part of that process is hunting, and part is resting, purring and sleeping.

Much of what we do is the same, although we don't realize it. Western culture promotes the hunt for financial gain. Yet it is interesting that those with the most money aren't the happiest; that honour goes to those who love what they do and the process.

Dreams of cats on the waning crescent moon are messages from Ishtar that your time to fight is done for now. It is time to put your feet up, tap into your femininity, and purr.

If the cat was hostile in your dream, you may meet hostility in your desire to take some time to yourself. But that is okay; they have their agenda, and you have yours. It is time to lay down your arms, curl up by the fire, and purr.

# Current Partners

If we stop to think about the word "partner", we quickly see past the assumption that we are talking about romantic, domestic life partners and notice that the term is far broader than that. Business partners, partners-in-crime, and partnerships with like-minded people and companies are some of the additional human partners we have in life. Partners come in all shapes and sizes and for all sorts of reasons.

Partnerships are mutually beneficial relationships. And once we open that door, we can start to appreciate that dreams about partners are dreams about relationships. Or, to be more precise, they are about how we feel about our relationships. It's Ishar's job to let us know there is a disturbance in our subconscious regarding our emotional connections. This information gets fed into our dreams, and our cognitive processes then try to put a face to it.

With this in mind, we should be able to see that a dream of, for example, infidelity should be taken seriously but not literally. What is infidelity? It's a betrayal of trust from a partner. Then it's our job to determine who the "partner" is and the nature of the betrayal. Framed this way, shady deals, family loyalties, rent increases, promotions, unexpected invoices and complaining neighbors suddenly come under scrutiny as fair game when we consider the meaning of our dream.

As usual, Ishar cares for our emotional balance. How we label them is not entirely in her control. How we interpret them is up to us. And *when* we have them can offer us more information.

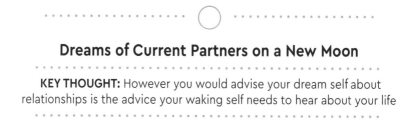

## Dreams of Current Partners on a New Moon

**KEY THOUGHT:** However you would advise your dream self about relationships is the advice your waking self needs to hear about your life

There are few things more exciting than the possibilities of a potential new relationship. Like the new moon, there's nothing tangible we can sink our teeth into with unrealized connections, only ethereal ideas, hopes and desires. That's what makes dreams of partners so interesting when they occur on the new moon.

Dreams of partners are dreams about relationships and, well, our relationship with relationships. It's important when analysing our dream to identify not the person in the dream but what they represent. We can look to the activities in the dream for clues.

Dining, doing housework, vacationing and paying for things together are all forms of interactions that may point to spiritual nourishment, work, desires, financial concerns, etc. And the tone of the interaction with our partner, be it collabourative, argumentative, easy or strained, can offer insight into how we feel about the facet of our lives Ishtar is bringing to our attention.

When we dream on the new moon, we sense that there are new opportunities that can be explored. And depending on our dream analysis, we can proceed with good information. If our analysis hints at a bumpy relationship with money, we can still proceed with financial commitments, but we may want to go over the budget one more time before we do. If we are dining happily with our partner, we can be confident that we are well nourished spiritually and, if we wish, have some latitude to take a few more risks as we have credit in our grounding.

When we dream of partners on the new moon, we are given the formula for our next steps. However we would advise our dream self about relationships is the advice our waking self needs to hear about our lives.

## Dreams of Current Partners
## on a Waxing Crescent Moon

**KEY THOUGHT:** Learn from the mistakes your dream self makes

The waxing crescent provides us an outline of what is to become of the moon in its coming phases, and, likewise, dreams on the waxing crescent hint at what we can expect, or believe we can expect, as we move through the subsequent phases of our lives.

Dreams of partners are reflections from our subconscious, psychic selves of what emotions we sense in our future. They can provide us with important information regarding our navigation of nascent activities.

And remember, dreams are not literal; they are symbolic. Our partners represent security, trust, reliance and mutually beneficial activities, and therefore dreams of partners might symbolize our deep feelings or concerns regarding anyone one of those.

It took me a long time to accept that the success or failure of a relationship was a success or a failure at all. I went through a phase of blaming and crediting the other. And I've been through phases of blaming or crediting myself. But Ishtar believes that's the wrong approach. She seeks opportunities to learn and grow.

While we cannot help, nor should we deny, our feelings, owning them should have nothing to do with our spiritual development. Learning from our relationships with our partners – either waking or in our dreams – is step one, and applying these lessons in our future activities is step two. The benefit of dream relationships is that there are no hurt feelings, only lessons to apply. It's as if they were mere simulations.

And that's what dreams of partners on the waxing crescent can offer us; pain-free life lessons from which we can grow.

## Dreams of Current Partners on a First Quarter Moon

**KEY THOUGHT:** Use your dream emotions to inform your decisions

Dreams of our current partners represent a snapshot of how we feel about one of the potentially many aspects of our lives. From financial concerns to security in the workplace, our relationships are many and complex. They are so complex, in fact, that we are often so blinded when in them that we cannot see what others see clearly. Likewise, how many of us have friends that seem oblivious to either the good or the bad in their lives that seem so clear to us?

Taking a step forward – or backward – can often upset the status quo of a relationship. From asking for a salary increase to deciding the book club is no longer for us, the scope of relationships we have and the reasons we might have for wanting more or less from them are numerous. But the anxiety we might feel making a step, in or out, can be paralyzing and is a nearly universal human experience. If only someone we trust could nudge us.

Dreams of partners on the first quarter moon are Ishtar's nudge. She is telling us that she sees the reality of our relationship with a specific facet of our lives and shows us what that looks and feels like. The rest is up to us.

The first quarter moon is a moon in transition, split between the shadow and the light. Denying our feelings is like living in shadow. Accepting the reality of our circumstances is like living in the light.

We cannot navigate in the dark and cannot make choices regarding our direction when living in shadow. Dreams of partners on the first quarter shine a light on our emotional state and provide us with the information we need to take our next step with confidence.

## Dreams of Current Partners
## on a Waxing Gibbous Moon

**KEY THOUGHT:** Ask for what you want. You might just receive it

The waxing gibbous moon and dreams that occur during its phase are both representations of ideas that are close to completion or perfection.

The details of the completion can often feel draining, as if it's the final push or regarded as not necessary given all the work that has been put into an endeavour. It should be recognized, however, that while no amount of wallpaper can fix shaky foundations, solid foundations can be built upon no matter the house's condition.

And dreams of partners on the waxing gibbous go one better than that. If all else is solid, the relationship may only need superficial, cosmetic attention. Ishtar is taking our current relationship as a metaphor for our life, prompting us to appreciate our solid foundations and nudging us to focus on better communication, openness, and honesty in situations we might feel burdened by.

If we are fatigued and unhappy at work, have we let our boss or HR know? If we are stressed about finances, have we done a review of costs, and are we living within our means? The perfect situation might be around the corner, but unless we ask where it is, we might walk past it.

Ask for what you want. You might just receive it.

## Dreams of Current Partners on the Full Moon

**KEY THOUGHT:** To everything, there is a season

I would like to float the idea of the three C's of friendship. Confidants are those who are on our side whether we are right or wrong. Like our mother and lifelong best friend, confidants will be there for us even if we change or screw up. Constituents are those that are for what we are for. In our journey in life, there may be times when we walk the same path, but that does not mean we have the same vision. Co-workers or running partners are examples. Comrades are against what we are against. We may link arms in protest or huddle in a doorway sheltering from a sudden rainstorm, but once the rain has stopped, we will go our separate ways.

If we are lucky, we might gain three or four confidants in our lifetime. The vast majority of our interactions are with those who are destined to be "merely" constituents or comrades. And there is nothing wrong with that. At the end of temporary employment, we shake hands and comment on how well that went. At the end of a football match, the players go home. The challenge for us is not to confuse constituents and comrades with confidants.

The vast majority of relationships we engage in have a time and a place, a season to bloom. Seeing the big picture and recognizing that most relationships are finite can turn a painful exit into a graceful acceptance that, in our journey in life, we had a good walking partner with whom to share the path for a time.

Dreams of partners on the full moon illuminate Ishtar's wisdom regarding our deeper feelings for our partner, employer, business partner, or perhaps even our running partner, and let us know that it's okay to be honest with how the relationship fits in our life garden.

To everything, there is a season.

## Dreams of Current Partners on a Waning Gibbous Moon

**KEY THOUGHT:** Forgive, but don't forget

Dreams of partners give us an opportunity to explore the complexities of human emotions without paying an entrance (or exit) fee. Personal relationships can be exciting, restrictive, sensual, rewarding, compromising, traumatizing and, sadly, abusive. Yet these descriptions can also apply to other facets of our life.

And as many of us know, life can be messy. Often, this phrase is used when we acknowledge someone's laps in judgement in personal matters. But Ishtar feels that any lapses in judgement are fair game to be labelled "messy".

In fact, dreams of partners on the waning gibbous moon are messages from our psyche that it's time to tweak, make a few changes, and deal with a little mess now before it overshadows all we do.

If I hear one more person say that love means never having to say you're sorry, I will seriously stick a tarot card in my eyeball. Forgiveness and moving on are essential in all areas of life, and I would like to take this moment to discuss that.

My favorite definition of "forgiveness" is "letting go of any hope for a better past". Many of us might think that forgiving someone for a transgression means we let them off the hook. But that's not what forgiveness means. I believe that it is a choice to release feelings of resentment, whether the person deserves it or not. Would we resent a snake for biting? Probably not. But we would be wise not to forget they bite.

When tidying up our life, the first and best way to remove emotional barriers and psychological toxins from our system is to forgive. If we resent the snake, we will fight it. If we forgive and remember, we can better handle the snake rationally without the venom of resentment coursing through our minds.

## Dreams of Current Partners on a Third Quarter Moon

**KEY THOUGHT:** Make healthy decisions at the end of play

There is good news, and then there is no news when we expect bad news. How palpable is the relief of no drama when drama is precisely what we expected?

Dreams of partners on the third quarter moon are Ishtar's way of letting us know that calling it a day should not be something to fear. Just as the moon, which was once bright and full, is now half concealed in shadow, many of our endeavours would benefit from recognizing its completion and be celebrated. There can be relief in letting go.

There is an English expression often voiced during the memorial of a beloved grandmother or grandfather. Derived from the game of cricket, an "inning" is the time a batsman can score runs – is in – before he makes a mistake and is "out". While making a mistake that ends his inning is not good news, it happens to all players sooner or later. And if a player scores a lot of runs before that happens, he is said to have had a good inning. Indeed, a player who scores over 100 runs receives a standing ovation immediately following the mistake that ended his play. He may be out, but he had a great inning.

Gratitude for what was can be a comforting consolation for loss. If Grandma lived to 86 before she passed, she had a great inning. If the business we started paid the bills for seven years before it folded, it had a great inning. And if a marriage lasted 15 years and brought happy kids into the world, there is value in that that should be acknowledged, not overshadowed by mistakes made near its end.

Dreams of partners on the third quarter moon encourage us to see the light and to make healthy decisions at the end of play.

## Dreams of Current Partners
## on a Waning Crescent Moon

**KEY THOUGHT:** Honour your past decisions,
even if they didn't turn out as you had hoped

The waning crescent moon presents us with a moment of resolution. I have talked a lot about resentment in this chapter. It's unfortunate that, for many of us, resentment echoes in the wake of relationships. That fact is testimony to the intensity of human emotions and the passions we invest in our connections with others. It also speaks to the missed opportunities for resolution.

Were this dream of partners to have come during the third quarter moon, my interpretation would be that Ishtar is calling us to be kind to others as we resolve and close a chapter. However, dreams on the waxing crescent speak of a more internal kindness.

Dreams of partners on this final phase symbolize our yearning for a gentle close to a facet of our endeavours that required collabouration with others. Regardless of the confusing emotions that often accompany such endings – sadness, remorse, anger or indifference – what we should remember, and what Ishtar is reminding us of, is that life is precious.

We have a finite number of days here. We should treasure and protect our state of mind. Honouring our past decisions as ones we thought were the best at the time does more for our self-esteem than chastising ourselves, or someone else, for not knowing something we could not have known then.

As a writer, I dislike trite expressions, but occasionally, I read ones I like. One that comes to mind is, "Love as if you've never been hurt." We can go a long way to removing, avoiding or healing our hurt feelings by holding onto the idea that we gave it our best shot, because that's all we can do.

# Death

Dreams about death can be traumatic, both within the dream and after waking. These "virtual" deaths may also, perversely, seem unimportant, dismissed or even giggled at during the dream – which can be even more disturbing when you wake up.

But here is the good news: dreams about death are dreams about *life*. You should trust that Ishtar has a positive, informed message. Though her symbolism may initially be upsetting – who wants to even think of death, let alone experience it, even in a dream? – you could do worse than take a leaf out of the Mesopotamian playbook when processing dreams of death. Their appreciation of death was that it is a spiritual passing rather than a physical one. If you focus on what Ishtar is trying to tell you (rather than indulge in the emotions you feel on waking), you stand a better chance of learning something important about your future growth.

If this book offers only one piece of advice, it would be that the most important aspect of a dream is how you feel in it, and also what the subject matter represents. The subject matter is symbolic, while the emotions are the truth.

For example, your mother represents your nurturing instincts, your spouse represents your openness to love, your children represent your legacy, and strangers represent anxiety toward the unknown. When you dream of death (or the threat of it), you must try to identify what the victim represents in your life and acknowledge how you felt about the death.

If you are offhand in your dream about witnessing the death of a loved one, you may want to consider taking yourself a little less seriously in matters of the heart. Perhaps your intensity may be putting undue stress on your relationships.

If you are the victim of the dream death, identifying the cause of death can direct you to the areas of life in which you have the opportunity to transform. Old leaves must fall from a tree's branches to ensure that there is room for new leaves to grow, and you must replace bad habits with good ones. While significant life decisions may feel drastic and terrifying at first, you know deep down that these are healthy in the long term. And that is what dreams of death are about: your long-term wellbeing.

## Dreams of Death on a New Moon

**KEY THOUGHT:** Don't hide your pain

In the physical world, birth means death is inevitable. In the spiritual realm, death means birth is inevitable. You must set sail to reach new shores, yet you can't appreciate arrival if you don't accept departure.

How often have you resolved to throw away junk in your home only to see new possibilities for newly emptied space (not to mention a few coins stuck between the cushions of the old sofa). It is like that with pain, too. Healthy grieving – accepting things have reached the end of their lifespan – is a critical part of healing. Denial only slows the process.

Dreams of death on the new moon are invitations sent by Ishtar to accept loss as an essential part of renewal. She is asking you to reflect on the end of a difficult period to allow peace back into your life. These dreams signify it is time to understand yourself, your reality and new opportunities.

A dull job, overwhelming finances or relationships that have past their expiry date are all areas that may gnaw at you over time. They erode your spirit, sometimes so slowly that you don't notice it. Yet if you *are* aware of it – or at least its potential and inevitability – you can insure against its insidious nature.

Diagnosis is the first step to healing. If you can quiet yourself and meditate on your present circumstances, you may be able to identify areas of discomfort. It takes honesty; some pain points may have significant consequences. If this is the case, you can just take one step at a time. But don't hide the pain.

And remember: in the spiritual realm, death means birth is inevitable.

## Dreams of Death on a Waxing Crescent Moon

**KEY THOUGHT:** Move on

As the sun's light begins to creep around the edge of the moon, it is natural to feel optimistic at the idea that light is coming, or, conversely, that shadow is lifting. Once the emotional shock you can sometimes experience after a dream of death has passed, you can, and should, frame dreams of death on the waxing crescent as exciting revelations of hope and transformation: shadows are lifting.

Transformation is challenging, and the older you are, the tougher it gets to change your ways. Often it takes a trauma – a passing of a loved one, divorce or the loss of a job – to inspire people to stop their self-destructive habits or at least help them see that they have them. But Ishtar doesn't feel you need to crash in order to learn. If you can channel the upset the dream may have caused and use it as fuel to effect change in your waking life, you may be able to avoid unnecessary hurt.

Look closely at how you felt in the dream, as this can indicate what Ishtar would like you to address. Indifference or distress in the dream represents your true feelings, and the victim or the circumstances show the aspect of your life that needs to go.

Any dream on the waxing crescent moon is a call to arms, and dreams of death are no exception. You must use this message to accept that there is an aspect of your life you want to put behind you. Only you can know what this may be, and only you can determine the first steps.

"First steps" is an apt expression. There are two ways to put something behind you: the hard way – changing the situation, person or thing itself – or the easy way – changing yourself; stepping in front of it, moving forward and leaving it behind.

Ishtar recommends the latter.

## Dreams of Death on a First Quarter Moon

**KEY THOUGHT:** Strike at the heart of antipathy lest
it be the death of you

Nothing is as decisive as death. Countless cultures throughout history have developed their own interpretation of the death event and the whereabouts of a soul that has passed. But there is no agreement or hard evidence to help us come to terms with its finality.

Crossing over from the light to the shadow is the moon's first quarter state, and the dream of death on the first quarter moon is all about turning uncertainty into certainty.

One thing *is* for certain; Ishtar speaks to you using symbolism. Your dream shouldn't be taken as literal; it is symbolic of your underlying desires, and you may need to unpack its details to better understand its meaning.

The death in your dream represents your subconscious desire to be done with an element of your life over which you are torn. To glean greater clarity, you need to connect the victim in the dream to a component of your life and recall how you felt about the death in the dream. This will determine your true feelings about that component of your waking life.

You may realize that you dislike your job or a friendship. You may learn that being the responsible one in the family is no longer satisfying and instead you wish to pursue artistic outlets. You may fear admissions, transitions or the conversations required to turn these ideas into reality, but that is your responsibility to manage, not Ishtar's. She is here to point out these tensions.

Whatever the root of the anxiety, dreams of death on the first quarter moon are unequivocal calls for you to turn the uncertainty of the light and shadow of the moon into the certainty of decisive, positive action. You must strike at the heart of antipathy to stop it becoming the emotional death of you.

## Dreams of Death on a Waxing Gibbous Moon

KEY THOUGHT: Cut the mooring rope if you wish to sail

In psychology, there is an action known as "killing the father". This is the final act of rebellion, usually by a male against his father, to become independent. From rejecting financial advice to pursuing radically different careers from their father, a child must shut down the last vestiges of parental control to enter adulthood.

In creative fields, there is an action known as "killing the baby". This refers to an artist being forced, through the creative process, to throw away a beloved initial idea for the greater good of a developing project.

Dreams of death on the waxing gibbous moon are a call from Ishtar to deal with the difficulties holding you back from fulfilling *your* desired goal. It may take some deeper analysis to look at what the victim and the cause of death represent in your psyche, but the general message couldn't be clearer; cut the mooring rope if you wish to sail in the long term.

. . . . . . . . . . . . . . . . . . . . . . ● . . . . . . . . . . . . . . . . . . . . . .

## Dreams of Death on a Full Moon

**KEY THOUGHT:** Give the seeds of your success water and time

Dreams of death on the full moon represent your deep desires to put an end to some facet of your personality that you feel is holding you back and plant seeds of renewal instead. Whether the dream death occurs or is just a threat, and regardless of the victim and the cause of death, you can regard the whole scene in your dream as your psyche being acted out by an ensemble cast and directed, of course, by Ishtar.

Much like a flower that blooms and disperses its seeds – an act that ensures both its legacy and its demise – the full moon timing of the dream informs you that you have rid yourself of shadow and are complete. Your seeds have been sown, and new life, new horizons and new opportunities are in motion.

While you may not yet see the seeds of these opportunities, you can be confident that the ingredients for your continued growth and success have been put in place.

All these now need is water and time.

## Dreams of Death on a Waning Gibbous Moon

**KEY THOUGHT:** Release the dead weight in your life

With the coming shadow now creeping over the waning moon, the waning gibbous phase is a sign of form in decline. Much like dusk, autumn or the threat of rain, the waning gibbous isn't a time for creativity but is for consolidation, packing up and the shedding of dead weight.

Dreams of death on the waning gibbous moon are messages from Ishtar that there is work to be done in the shedding of that dead weight, and she knows what that work is.

The dream of death isn't a literal suggestion; it is a stage play of your psyche, with each actor representing a component of your psychic self. Whether this is your love life, finances or job, the death in your dream, the victim and the cause of death point to what your subconscious thinks is holding you back and advises you to "deal with".

Determining the specifics of your dream is the work of the dreamer. If you consider the role of the victim, you can assign them to a part of your life, and the cause of death also offers perspective. Think it through.

As personal as the specifics are, the general message is clear: you must begin to release the dead weight in your life.

## Dreams of Death on a Third Quarter Moon

**KEY THOUGHT:** Burn down the old to make space for the new

Dreams of death can shock the system. The good news is that these aren't literal and that the death (or the threat of it) can offer pointers to areas of your life that it is time to put to rest.

Dreams on the third quarter moon tell you that, as the shadows close in and split the moon into equal parts, light and shade, you are split and must make decisions about your future. In dreams of death on the third quarter moon, Ishtar is encouraging you to close a chapter and leap, even if you are unsure what the next chapter has in store for you.

It is uncertain, but this is the point. The new door won't open *until* the first door is closed. The net won't appear *until* you leap.

Forests rejuvenate after a forest fire because some seeds, dormant for years, are activated by the heat of the fire. Dreams of death on the third quarter moon are exactly this.

You must burn down the old to make space for the new.

## Dreams of Death on a Waning Crescent Moon

**KEY THOUGHT:** Few things last forever.
Be grateful for the moments you had

As the darkness begins to literally overshadow the light of the sun reflected off the moon, it is time to tidy up and put things away. Contrary to the emotional shock you may experience when you wake from a dream about death, you are being offered an opportunity for peace and closure.

Few things in your experience last your entire lifetime. If you have two or three lifelong friends, you are blessed. If you can accept that all else – most other people, your job, your career, friends, living situations, pets, experiences, loves, resentments, good fortune and bad luck – are merely fleeting, you will suffer less as you ride the rollercoaster of life.

Dreams of death on the waning crescent give you an opportunity and a reminder to be grateful for the light you have received even as you draw the curtains on it.

# Dogs

Few things represent loyalty, protection and companionship better than our relationship with dogs. It is well documented that dogs lower stress levels and improve our wellbeing. Commonplace expressions such as licking one's wounds attest to the health benefits our canine friends offer us.

Generally, dog dreams allow you to hear what Ishtar says about your friendship and emotional wellbeing. Even angry dogs, unless rabid, are typically associated with protection – of you, its owner, its territory, etc. – and should be regarded not as hostile but as expressions of loyalty and love: positive messages.

The timing of your dog dream can inspire you to examine nuances you rarely prioritize in your everyday life.

## Dreams of Dogs on a New Moon

**KEY THOUGHT:** Plan your ideal garden of relationships

The new moon is the fertile ground in which to plant the seeds you wish to grow in your life garden. And just as importantly, it is a time to identify what you do *not* want to encourage, to ensure you don't perpetuate self-sabotaging relationships.

Recognize the dream as a message to take an inventory of your desires. Use this moment as inspiration and ask yourself, "What do I want my future friendship circle to look like? What do I want? What do I not want?"

Seize this moment to plan your future life garden and start sowing the right seeds. You don't yet need to act upon these ideas; the timing of this dream indicates that your subconscious is yearning for you to "take stock" and identify opportunities. This is a time to be honest with yourself and ask questions such as:

"Which of my relationships are working? What is it about them that I like? What do I want more of in my life?"

"Which of my relationships are *not* working? What is it about them that I *don't* like? What do I want *less* of in my life?"

Write your ideas down.

## Dreams of Dogs on a Waxing Crescent Moon

**KEY THOUGHT:** Pursue intriguing new relationships

The waxing crescent is the first flower of a new spring, an optimistic yet fragile icon of the desires you must try to nurture and protect. Just as the gardener may experience an early frost when nurturing seeds, dreams of cogs on the waxing crescent moon are a call to action to safeguard fledgling relationships. If you wish to bring positivity, love and friendship into your life, you must support these wishes with positive action.

Use the timing of the dog dream as inspiration to remember your relationship goals and have the courage and belief to stay the course on your journey. There is work to do – joyful work – and now is *not* the time to quit relationships you want to nurture.

If there is a chase in your dream – even if the dog is doing the chasing – this should be interpreted as encouragement to pursue elusive friendships or business connections. But if the dog in your dream is aggressive or out of control, this could signify that you are involved in unhealthy pursuits. Take this moment to identify harmful relationships and distance yourself from them.

## Dreams of Dogs on a First Quarter Moon

**KEY THOUGHT:** Reflect on how you can "get out of your own way" with relationships

Since the hard angle of the moon in its first quarter moon represents transition, this phase can manifest as doubt and may test your confidence or commitment: Are you in or out?

Dreams of dogs on the first quarter offer a glimpse into deep concerns. Ishtar is challenging you to consider your beliefs in your relationship goals. Use this moment to seek out where you may tend to feel negative emotions – such as defeatism or pride – that erode the quality of your connections with others.

Now is an excellent time to reflect on your ego's role in helping or hindering your journey to more fulfilling personal relationships.

## Dreams of Dogs on a Waxing Gibbous Moon

**KEY THOUGHT:** Seek ways to fine-tune and
deep well-established friendships

Bulging with potential, dreams of dogs on the waxing gibbous moon are a sure sign that you are bountiful in the opportunities you have with your connection to others, even if these are not yet fully formed. You should recognize your relationships as works in progress.

Following dreams of dogs on the waxing gibbous moon, you may wish to take a moment to tweak, hone and adjust – fine-tune – your actions in the pursuit of a more perfect life journey.

No two relationships are alike: each requires unique care and maintenance. You can take your dream as your unconscious calling to review your closest connections with your loved ones. Then you can ask yourself:

"What small change could I make to be a better friend/wife/husband to this other person," and, equally importantly, "What small change could I ask of another that would eliminate misunderstandings and enrich my connection with this person?"

## Dreams of Dogs on a Full Moon

**KEY THOUGHT:** Accept the limits of challenging relationships, and don't take the challenges personally

Given the high emotion and energy of the full moon, dreams of dogs during this phase can serve to remind you that if lovers or friends challenge you, this may be due to unhelpful emotions in other areas of their life and you shouldn't assume it is personal. Just as you may take a taxi home after drinking a few glasses of wine at a restaurant, Ishtar may be pointing out that taking a moment of pause before you act impulsively may be the best course of action for you and the relationship.

Use the opportunity of the dog on the full moon to practice mindfulness, take a breath and appreciate the beauty of the moment without acting on fuelled emotions.

You can also take a moment to accept that some relationships may have reached their peak. While this may feel disappointing (if you had hoped for more), it can also be a time to appreciate what you have, soften your ego and count your blessings.

## Dreams of Dogs on a Waning Gibbous Moon

**KEY THOUGHT:** If you could prune your circle of friendship, consider where you might trim

Just as the waxing lunar phase focuses on nurturing the positive, its waning phase can provide inspiration to trim the negative.

Dreams of dogs on the waning gibbous moon are unambiguous messages that trimming, pruning and removing harmful or toxic influences may be in order. This is the perfect moment to take an inventory of friendships and identify hurtful, stale, cursed or malignant connections.

This doesn't mean that you necessarily need to sever ties and act hastily. The first step to healing is to recognize the problem, and it seems that Ishtar is speaking up.

Dreams of dogs on the waning gibbous moon are messages that encourage you to spend a kind moment with yourself, practice honest awareness and bring to your conscious minds things you may wish to address at some point in the future.

While a journey of a thousand miles begins with a single step, the step can't happen unless you know you want to take it. And that is what this moment is about: awareness.

## Dreams of Dogs on a Third Quarter Moon

**KEY THOUGHT:** Distance yourself from toxicity

Astrologically, the moon's third quarter is a power struggle that manifests itself in conflict. Dreams of dogs at this time are vivid and unmistakable messages of caution and action.

Use this knowledge to take stock of any conflict, resistance or disagreements in your life and recognize that you are not always in complete control. Some things are simply out of your hands.

If you accept that it takes two to tango, you can start to disconnect from other, self-destructive thought processes such as powerlessness, frustration, self-blame and, ultimately, anger, and begin to move toward a healthier outlook.

Just as you can distance yourself from your own negative processes, you can, and should, do the same when met with negativity from others. There are ways to do this without inciting conflict. If you avoid taking the proper steps for yourself out of fear that it may provoke a confrontation, this is a more serious issue. You may need help in these situations. Only you can know the truth, and it is up to you to take your emotions seriously.

When you can surrender to the things that are not in your control, you take a step toward serenity. Note that there is a difference between the serenity of accepting the reality that you are in a toxic relationship and putting up with it.

## Dreams of Dogs on a Waning Crescent Moon

**KEY THOUGHT:** Seek to heal through dialogue,
forgiveness or simply letting go

No matter the attitude or behaviour of the dog in your waning crescent dream, you have an opportunity to find healing and positive guidance in this message.

Generally, dog dreams in this phase may inspire you to review relationships that require some TLC. You are too busy, and life is too hectic, for you to ponder these challenging things on a daily basis. But here and now, you can trust that Ishtar has your back and has prompted you for good reason. She believes it is important, and you should heed the prompt.

One particularly interesting and counterintuitive sub-category of dog dreams on the waning crescent moon is the aggressive dog. While it may be tempting to be cautious, the waning crescent's positive nature tells you something different. Consider that "aggressive" may also mean "competitive", representing friendship with someone who thrives on ambition and success.

Take a moment to think about what that may mean for you.

# Ex-partners

Ishtar always sees the big picture. There is no past or future for her; she has access to it all, but not in material detail. She sees *emotional* contour, so when you dream of ex-partners, Ishtar is speaking not of your ex-partners but your present desires.

For most people to move on with their life, ex-partners have to be filed away as "over". But in the symbolic world of your subconscious, the image of your ex fits into categories of love, support, intimacy, nostalgia and perhaps jealousy, pain, betrayal and loss. In the waking world, the relationship may be over, but in Ishtar's world these emotions are reference points.

When you dream of ex-partners, the ex represents the *feelings*, not the person. These may be ones you are experiencing in waking life – that Ishtar is relating to as you dream – or these may be your desires that Ishtar is nudging you to pursue.

As you journey through life, you can fall in love, fall *out* of love, get *pushed* out of love or seek *new* love. The feelings are powerful and often confusing. You may be busy socially yet emotionally lonely. You may be in a personal relationship that is almost-but-not-quite perfect yet yearn for that missing piece. These conflicting desires, while impractical (and probably unreasonable), are also unavoidable, and your subconscious seeks ways to reconcile them.

When Ishtar gets wind of that, you should expect an informed opinion from her.

# Dreams of Ex-partners on a New Moon

**KEY THOUGHT:** Don't call the ex-*partner*, recall the ex-*feeling*, and consider how to meet up with that

When you dream on the new moon, you open yourself up to the message from Ishtar that there is a blank slate before you on which you can carve your future. The shadows of uncertainty will be pushed back by the four D's; desire, decisiveness, determination and details. On the new moon, it is time to identify your desire.

When you dream of an ex-partner, you are being nostalgic about the security you felt. Now isn't the time to reflect on the ups and downs of a past love; it is time to accept that the feelings that were present in *that* relationship are ones you yearn for at *this* moment.

It is important to see the difference between legitimately wanting those feelings and thinking that this person in your past can provide them. If you ask yourself, "What was the best thing I felt during that relationship?", you stand a good chance of identifying the emotion you long for in your present waking life.

If you can avoid calling the ex-partner and, instead, recall the ex-*feeling*, you make the first move toward a beautiful reunion.

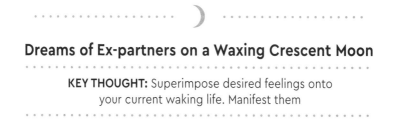

# Dreams of Ex-partners on a Waxing Crescent Moon

**KEY THOUGHT:** Superimpose desired feelings onto your current waking life. Manifest them

Dreams of ex-partners can evoke many confusing and conflicting emotions. One way to make the dream interpretation easier is to separate the person from the feelings and then focus on the feelings.

The waxing crescent is a time of emerging reality gradually coming into focus, pushing back the doubt's high tide and replacing it with concrete manifestation. With dreams of your ex-partner broadcast into your awareness during this lunar phase, this can be a challenging waking moment.

Take a moment to reflect on your current waking life and superimpose on it the feelings – not the person – you enjoyed (or not) in your dream. If you are honest with yourself, you should be able to see an alignment of emotional imagery with the dream emotion filling gaps in your current waking life.

Manifestation – picturing what you desire – is an ancient and widely known technique to bring your desires to reality. Drawing a desired home, writing of a desired love and praying for a desired outcome are well-documented practices of the faithful. The same laws apply to displaying emotional outcomes.

By superimposing your desires onto your walking emotional landscape, as you would dress a doll, you manifest for your future more of the pleasures you have experienced in your past. This means you take a step closer to your better self.

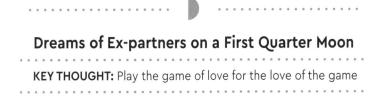

## Dreams of Ex-partners on a First Quarter Moon

**KEY THOUGHT:** Play the game of love for the love of the game

The bargain of life is made up of emotional gains and also the emotional price you pay for those gains. The currency with which you bargain is love. As the saying goes: it is better to have loved and lost than never to have loved at all. To be in the business of love is to be in the business of love *gained* and *lost*.

There are choices, though. To live a life guarded against love *lost* is one option, yet stepping away from the game of love is, in a deep sense, stepping away from the game of *life*. To live a life vacant of the gains and losses that love can provide – and you can't have the former without a high probability of the latter – is to miss most of the dynamics of life.

Dreams of ex-partners on the first quarter moon are Ishtar's way of reminding you of the full scope of life and encouraging you to play the game of love, for the love of the game.

## Dreams of Ex-partners on a Waxing Gibbous Moon

**KEY THOUGHT:** Fine-tune new love with lessons learned

Dreams of ex-partners are about the *feelings* the relationship evoked. You can't know a day until you have seen the sun both rise *and* set, you can't know the moon until you have seen the lunar cycle in full, and you can't truly know love until you see all its seasons. Spring and summer don't make a year. Only the loss of love can teach you its true value – the valley defines the peak. Only past relationships contain this message in full.

Dreams of ex-partners on the waxing gibbous moon are messages from Ishtar to recall and appreciate the rich scope of relationships and apply your wisdom to your *present* waking life.

Why is it better to have loved and lost than never to have loved? Surely it is better to have loved and not lost. Yet, how can you appreciate the value of light if you haven't experienced the dark – of the luxury of health if you haven't suffered ill health? Similarly, experiencing and learning from loss can teach you the value of love and the stakes at play. Only then can you grow, mature and fine-tune new love with lessons learned.

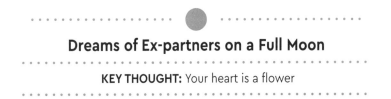

## Dreams of Ex-partners on a Full Moon

**KEY THOUGHT:** Your heart is a flower

Only love that has run its course can show you the full scope of your emotional capacity. From the excitement and passion of the springtime of new love to the verdant security of summer, the melancholia of autumn as leaves begin to fall, to the bleak and dormant winter of reflection and renewal, the cycle of love prepares for springtime again.

To have faith that love *is* a cycle of seasons (not some linear "forever" notion that either succeeds or fails) is to accept consciously what every other species and the plant kingdom already know: your purpose is to grow and the seasons of love are there to help you do that.

Dreams of ex-partners on the full moon are Ishtar's reminder that your heart is a flower.

## Dreams of Ex-partners on a Waning Gibbous Moon

**KEY THOUGHT:** Let your leaves fall with grace

As the shadows of the waning gibbous moon begin to creep across what was, only days ago, a brilliant full moon, you can liken the encroaching doubt as the herald to its demise.

Anyone who has loved and lost will have gained priceless wisdom in matters of the heart. While you may not have recognized shadow beginning to shade your past love at the time, only ex-relationships can provide the requisite hindsight to see where and when its waning began.

Dreams of ex-partners on the waning gibbous moon remind you that there is a season to everything, and even if it is the melancholy of a relationship in its autumn months, each season is essential if you are to grow. Maybe some people come into your life for a season or a reason or maybe for life. Just like the moon, life and love have cycles. The part any love plays in your life story is precisely that: a *part*. Sometimes, no matter how much effort you invest in holding onto a relationship that was only ever meant to be for a season, you are only trying to hold back the tides of change. Better to let it raise your boat than sink your spirit.

You may fret, blame, rage or accuse when relationships begin to fail. This is understandable, especially if you feel you have been wronged. Yet if you can recognize – as painful as it may be – that the "wrong" is a *symptom* of autumn not its *cause*, you can be grateful for when the sun did shine on you, trust that it will shine again, and let your leaves fall with grace.

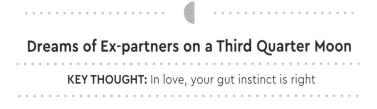

## Dreams of Ex-partners on a Third Quarter Moon

**KEY THOUGHT:** In love, your gut instinct is right

Few things are more noble than fighting for what is right, fighting for love and committing, investing and forgiving in matters of the heart. It is even more poetic when both parties work through stormy times.

Yet, as most people who have loved and lost will know, you can only try so hard before you know deep down that a relationship is over on an emotional level. You can act like it isn't, pretend to yourself, other people and your social circle that you are "all good". But Ishtar knows when the light has gone out; if you are honest with yourself, you do too.

Dreams of ex-partners on the third quarter moon are reminders from Ishtar to be honest with yourself in matters of the heart, and this applies not just to your lovers. Your intuition is a skilled and nuanced adviser if only you would trust it. From handshake deals to choosing a house to purchase, your gut instinct is usually right. Typically, your regrets stem, for the most part, from moments when you don't listen to your intuition.

## Dreams of Ex-partners on a Waning Crescent Moon

**KEY THOUGHT:** Accept loss not as failure but as nourishment

Many people may be aware of the notion of soulmates, love (and diamonds) being forever, and the idea that lost love is somehow a failure. And this is a shame.

If you were to ask your elders how many friends they have had in their life compared to those they regard as lifelong, or how many jobs they had, or homes, hopes or loves, you could probably predict the answer: many.

Most things in life are temporary. That isn't to say these are vacuous or meaningless, or if they are, they would be as vacuous as a rain shower to a spring bloom.

Dreams of ex-partners on the waning crescent moon are reminders from Ishtar that, while few things in life are permanent, all experiences in life nourish you. If you accept loss as nourishment rather than as failure, you will be fresher for it.

# Falling

By a show of hands, who here has never fallen? ... Yeah, I thought so. I did it just a few weeks ago. Not looking where I was walking, my foot went into a pothole, and before I knew what had happened, I was going down. I have vivid recollections of knowing that I was wiping out, and, worse, knowing that I did not have time even to put my arms out: I was in mid-fall, out of control, and unable to prevent the inevitable bumpy landing.

Thankfully, no damage was done. The experience was a visceral example of what dreams of falling represent: lack of control. And as with all else in Ishtar's world, she recognizes these subconscious feelings of lack of control, direction, security and achievement and reflects them back via our dream state. And that's where our cognitive processes interpret the data. If it feels like falling, it must be because we *are* falling, and there the picture is painted, and the dream is experienced.

Feelings of loss of control, falling behind, operating at maximum capacity while fearful of making a mistake, insecurity and awareness of danger are all the possible root causes of the emotions that can produce these dreams.

And as always, Ishtar has our back and lets us know that defensive instincts lurk in our subconscious, which we should be aware of and take seriously. If we can see the dream of falling not for what it looks like but for what it suggests, we have an opportunity to tweak our life choices in a healthier direction.

And what is the preventative cure for falling? Balance. If we fall, we lack balance. If we dream of falling, we lack balance in our life even if we do not recognize it in our waking state. Now is the time to find the cause of our imbalance, and if we look at when in the lunar cycle the dream occurred, we can gain greater insight into where we can seek it.

## Dreams of Falling on a New Moon

**KEY THOUGHT:** Get out of your own way

The new moon is a time for creativity and endless possibilities. And dreams on the new moon indicate similar spiritual optimism. So, on the surface, it seems quite incongruous that we dream of falling, suggesting that things feel out of our control. But Ishtar has her reasons, and a little digging and self-reflection can help.

In life, we get to know our playing style and act – we would like to think – according to our strengths. We apply for the positions for which we feel best suited. We speak up when we believe we have good information to share. And conversely, those who can't swim don't go in the water. We tend to avoid things we believe are not our strengths. We never do those things, so hence never improve at them. Years down the line, we simply don't consider taking responsibility for something that, in our adult life, we may be perfectly capable of achieving yet rule out due to some ghost of the past.

Dreams of falling on the new moon are messages from Ishtar that, in the areas of creativity, initiation and conception of plans, we might feel underdeveloped or utilized. It's a yearning that we clearly care about and are passionate about pursuing. We may lack confidence, but let's put that to rest. Do you think a baby has confidence in learning languages? It's a silly question. Confidence has nothing to do with it. Confidence is our natural state. Only when we grow do we invent reasons to lack it.

Ishtar believes we should just get out of our own way and do what we desire. And I agree with her; we should get out of our own way.

## Dreams of Falling on a Waxing Crescent Moon

**KEY THOUGHT:** Attend all your life's planning sessions

As the waxing crescent hints its form, our subconscious relates this in its own way to the ideas, endeavours and relationships we are embarking on and shares optimism for the future.

And while the early days of any idea in development are ripe with opportunity, it is a critical time for us to be sure the big decisions are pointing in the right direction.

When we dream of falling, we have a chance to consider where in our creative and entrepreneurial expressions we are making big decisions. We should not concern ourselves with details yet. Just as we don't pick a hotel before we decide what kind of holiday we desire, being sure we speak up and have some say over our direction in life is Ishtar's intention.

Dreams of falling on the waxing crescent moon are messages to attend all our life's planning sessions.

# Dreams of Falling on a First Quarter Moon

**KEY THOUGHT:** It's never too late to say, "This is my stop"

Just as the first quarter moon struggles to find its identity, so does our subconscious as it wrestles with inner dilemmas. When we dream of falling on the first quarter moon, Ishtar is telling us that we should stay keenly aware of whose ideas we invest in and focus on what we want for ourselves.

A business coach once told me that if I did not work toward my vision of the future, I would end up working toward someone else's. And Ishtar is offering a similar caution with dreaming of falling. She is suggesting that we are losing control of our journey, losing our grip on our vision, and feeling insecure about whether the endeavours we are working on are what we want for ourselves.

There is no shame in nipping things in the bud when we realize they are not what we want. In fact, there is strength in owning that kind of awareness. We know it in our gut when something is not for us. Being honest about "not feeling it" not only releases a lot of tension for us internally, but it's also the best thing for the work or the people from whom we are stepping away.

It's never too late for us to say, "This is my stop."

# Dreams of Falling on a Waxing Gibbous Moon

**KEY THOUGHT:** Don't forget to put a bow on it

While, proverbially speaking, it is darkest just before dawn, the waxing gibbous promises a sunny day ahead once the details are completed.

Dreams of falling allude to inner feelings of lack of control, guidance or confidence. Yet, with the waxing gibbous' promise of a bright day so near at hand, now is a critical time for us to finish what we have started, have the faith that we are on track, and reclaim control of the projects in our life that need our attention to their details.

Finishing touches are, fairly or not, the things that others notice, comment on, and that our feelings of worth can often rely on. Literally and figuratively speaking, putting the icing on the cake is what makes cakes get invitations to every party. The icing is 10% of the work and gets 90% of the applause.

When we dream of falling on the waxing gibbous moon, Ishtar is concerned that we are feeling that we are not attending to or valuing as much as we know we should, the presentation of the things we have worked so hard to achieve.

Don't forget to put a bow on it.

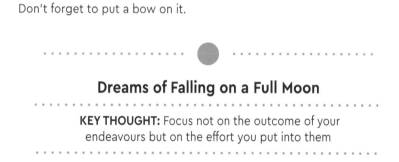

## Dreams of Falling on a Full Moon

**KEY THOUGHT:** Focus not on the outcome of your endeavours but on the effort you put into them

NASA's "vomit comet" is a seatless plane used to train astronauts. The idea is that, just as a thrown ball travels in a parabolic arc, a plane flying on the same arc will cause those within the plane to appear to "float". There is no magic, of course. They just have the trajectory of a thrown ball, as does the plane, and gravity is taken out of equations. When everything falls, nothing falls. The sensation of falling is the same as the sensation of weightlessness. It's all a matter of perspective.

Dreams of falling on the full moon can, in some way, be a terrifying omen. It might seem that dreams of falling – alluding to feelings of loss of direction or control – could not have come at a worse time. The full moon is a time of peak energy, light and wholeness, and all the psychological analogies that accompany it. Loss of control and direction at the moment of completion sounds like bad news. But it does not have to be. It's a matter of perspective.

By accepting that things may not always go as planned, that there are forces outside of our control that can influence the outcome, and that despite less than 100% results, we know we put in 100% effort, we shift from free-fall to weightlessness.

Even NASA's astronauts end up back on the ground, and no one can accuse them of a zero net gain. Staking our self-esteem not on the outcome of our endeavours but the effort we put into them will shift our perspective from free-fall to weightlessness and the lightness of being.

## Dreams of Falling on a Waning Gibbous Moon

**KEY THOUGHT:** The more frequently you attend to your emotional balance, the less dramatic any adjustments need to be

As the waning gibbous moon marks the turning of the lunar high tide, it still shines bright even as its power, size, illumination and psychic influence begin to recede. It heralds a time of consolidation and putting things in order.

And dreams of falling are suggestions from Ishtar that we are subconsciously stressed and feeling out of control of things in our lives. There are hints that things are out of balance and need to be addressed.

A tight-rope walker has much at stake when he steps out into the void. His life depends on his balance. Yet when we watch him walk, we do not see him flail. He walks slowly and deliberately, and if his instincts feel off-balance, he makes minor adjustments. The more frequently he attends to his balance, the less dramatic the adjustments need to be.

I sometimes feel pressure or imbalance about finances. Not because I am in a dire situation; more because I have neglected to look at them.

I then "free-fall" and spiral until dreadful, if not irrational emotions preoccupy me. Yet all it takes is 15 minutes a week for me to review my expenses, and all that emotion dissipates. And if I do that every week, things never really go that far off track.

The more frequently we attend to our emotional balance, the less dramatic any adjustments need to be. And when we dream of falling on the waning gibbous moon, Ishtar is nudging us to take care of the little things, so we stay balanced on the rope.

## Dreams of Falling on a Third Quarter Moon

**KEY THOUGHT:** When you close doors softly,
others will open effortlessly

The third quarter moon is a dramatic and tense time in the lunar cycle, emanating a sense of demise. Of course, the moon is not in demise, it is a cycle of waxing and waning, but without a full understanding of all its phases and how they work, it might *feel* that way.

As it is with sky-diving: the thrill seeker who jumps out of a plane does not regard the opening of his parachute as the end of his fun as much as he sees it as a guarantee that he can do it again.

Dreams of falling on the third quarter moon are messages from Ishtar to keep perspective when things feel like they are coming to a close. As surely as the leaves fall from the trees, spring is on its way. And as any gardener will know, the best return on the investment of time in the garden is the work done in the autumn. He who clears in November will have more control in May. When we dream of falling, Ishtar is addressing feelings of lack of control. And this control is arguably more powerfully manifested in the way we close the shop than in how we open it.

Settling debts, ending relationships honourably, and leaving jobs gracefully, are all ways we can ensure good fortune in the future. When we close doors softly, others will open effortlessly.

## Dreams of Falling on a Waning Crescent Moon

**KEY THOUGHT:** Don't go to bed angry

As the waning crescent moon fades, we naturally feel it is time to resolve any outstanding issues that feel unsettled or leave us unbalanced. And this desire for balance dovetails with dreams of falling, which allude to feelings of loss of control, direction and balance.

I believe there are two types of people in the world; those who are okay leaving for work without making their bed and those who would not feel comfortable all day if they did not make it. For better or worse, I make my bed. I leave other things messy, but the bed has to be made. Joking aside, most of us have something habitual we do that, if left untended to, would leave us feeling unsettled. And on a spiritual level, this is what I want us to consider when we dream of falling on a waning crescent moon.

Even if we are unaware of our habits, there may be things that unbalance us unless we address them. Knowing what these are, and putting in the work to see them done, can elevate much of our subconscious stress. And if you don't believe me, ask Ishtar. Our dream of falling on the waning crescent moon is all about our desire to ease stress by taking control of the loose ends of our lives so that, come the new day – and the new moon – our perspective is uncluttered.

And this is not confined to making beds. Any emotional upset is up for resolution. To wrap it up nicely, we should strive never to go to bed angry.

# Fish

Generally, fish are so removed from humans and live in such an alien and inhospitable (though often alluring) environment that it is almost impossible to relate to them. The "culture" (if you can call it that) of undersea life is incredibly hostile. It is a dog-eat-dogfish world down there. There is no place for empathy in the ocean, and other than a few exceptions – such as dolphins, whales, turtles, etc. – humans have little compassion for them.

Fish are elegant and savage, social and solitary, the hunter and the hunted, and numerous beyond imagining. They are unknowable. What we *do* know is we have to be crafty to catch them, they nourish us and when they rot they become uniquely foul.

They represent a tricky dilemma: desired nourishment at a cost. Fish are untrustworthy: they bait and bite; they are suspicious; they are supremely skilled when in water and desperate for help when out of it – literally, a fish out of water.

Dreams of fish are complex messages from Ishtar that you must be careful in what you set bait for and those that set bait for you.

(There is some correlation between fish dreams and pregnancy. While this is well documented and worthy of mention, this chapter will remain more general. Additionally, dreams of sharks have very specific interpretations worth addressing – there is a chapter dedicated to them in this book.)

## Dreams of Fish on a New Moon

**KEY THOUGHT:** Know what you wish to catch before you bait your hook

There is an expression in business that refers to a unique idea in an uncontested market. A Blue Ocean strategy identifies opportunity in a place where no other land is in sight, and dreams on the new moon are much like this: pure possibility.

Dreams of fish on the new moon are a message from Ishtar that, no matter how you may feel, there are, as they say, plenty of fish in the sea. If you can identify your blue ocean, you can have your pick. Yet while the idea of a blue ocean sounds refreshing, you must remember that although its surface may be calm, reflecting a clear sky, beneath its mercurial shimmer lurks mercurial minds.

When you pursue opportunity, whether this is money, a partner, etc., you may need to use bait. In pursuit of money, your bait may be the offer of services or the sale of material goods. In pursuit of a partner, the bait may be . . . well, this is most interesting.

There are many reasons why you may seek a partner. A dance partner, a life partner, and a casual sex partner are all partners of a kind, but the bait you would use for each of these would vary wildly. This is what Ishtar is guiding you to consider.

One of my favorite sayings is: If we give a man a fish, we feed him for a day, but if we *teach* him to fish, we feed him for a *lifetime*. One of the most important things about fishing is knowing how to bait your desires.

Before you bait your hook, you must know what you wish to catch.

## Dreams of Fish on a Waxing Crescent Moon

**KEY THOUGHT:** Dive into the ocean of your desires

The waxing crescent is a time for acting on your desires. Just as the light of the sun moves to expose areas of the moon's surface, the movement of the earth and the pull of the moon conspire to create the ocean's tides, which, in turn, hide and expose rockpools that teem with life.

When light, the ocean or your imagination expose and inspire new goals, you have fresh fields of play if only you embrace them.

You can't catch fish without getting wet, you can't enjoy the view without climbing the hill and you can't explore the beauty of the coral reefs without holding your breath. There is always a price to pay for the things you desire. Dreams of fish on the waxing crescent moon are an invitation from Ishtar to dive into the ocean of your desires and fish.

The purpose of the angler isn't *the catch* – it is *the fishing*. The catch is the consequence. It is the same with your goals. Your purpose isn't your *achievement*; it is your *endeavour*. Your success is the consequence.

## Dreams of Fish on a First Quarter Moon

**KEY THOUGHT:** Reel in opportunities

The craft of fishing is 99 per cent patience. And after that, it is all about speed and decisiveness.

Dreams of fish on the first quarter moon are about reeling in opportunities. You can have all the patience in the world, but if you can't, won't or don't pull the fishing rod at the right time, you will miss every time.

This "reeling in opportunities" doesn't need to be as dramatic as catching prey. Turning up on time, proofreading your job application email and sticking to a fitness regimen are all examples of reeling in.

You may not necessarily catch every time, but if you don't try to reel in any bite you get, you will catch nothing.

## Dreams of Fish on a Waxing Gibbous Moon

**KEY THOUGHT:** When you trawl for opportunities, be sure your net is fit to catch them

Putting concerns of ocean depletion and industrial-scale overfishing aside for one moment, the small fishing-village aesthetic can be beautiful and its characters fascinating. They respect the ocean, know their craft and maintain their tools. One particularly ironic task of their maintenance is the fixing of holes in their nets. If the holes are too small, they will catch without discretion. If the holes are too big, they will be wasting their time. Even if the holes are a perfect size, except for one large rip, the entire endeavour is wasted.

Fixing holes in your net is an essential task. Dreams of fish on the waxing gibbous moon are not just about trawling for life's opportunities. This is about ensuring that you have prepared appropriately to catch them.

## Dreams of Fish on a Full Moon

**KEY THOUGHT:** Don't release the good in
the hope of netting the perfect

Fisherman's tales are tall stories, exciting but questionable – "the one that got away".

Yet, "the one that got away" has also become synonymous with bragging, eyerolls, and trumped-up fantasies. Because, in truth, until you see the one that got away, you can't know for sure.

Dreams of fish on the full moon are signs from Ishtar that, for all the fish in the sea – for all the opportunities out there – the only useful ones are those you can see. Or, to paraphrase an airborne proverb, a fish in your net is worth two in your wishes.

You shouldn't release *the good* in the hope of netting *the perfect*. You should hold onto the good and keep on fishing.

## Dreams of Fish on a Waning Gibbous Moon

**KEY THOUGHT:** Be tenacious, but don't be obsessive

There is a saying where I come from; fish and friends go bad after three days. The idea is, for those who are unfamiliar, no matter how comfortable a host makes you feel, you shouldn't outstay your welcome.

The professional angler knows two things instinctively: when to cast their line and when to cut their losses. Dreams of fish on the waning gibbous have a similar intention; awareness of when to let go and drop the pursuit.

The pursuit of any goal often needs a degree of tenacity, but for the hunter, tenacity shouldn't be confused with, or morph into, obsessiveness. When Ishtar shows you visions of fish on the waning gibbous moon, she is cautioning you that the shadow of obsessiveness may be obscuring your objectivity.

## Dreams of Fish on a Third Quarter Moon

**KEY THOUGHT:** Choose achievable goals over wishful thinking

Dreams of fish on the third quarter moon are Ishtar's way of cautioning that you may have bitten off more than you can handle and hooked more than you can land.

In pursuit of happiness, money, goals, partners and adventure, most people cast a wide net. Anyone with any life experience will know a low percentage of endeavours succeed precisely as desired. This then becomes a numbers game; the wider the net – the more you try – the more success you should have. Yet this numbers game can sometimes be blinding.

Someone who spends all their time trying to reel in the big fish only to have their line eventually snap may exhaust the energy and time that could have been better spent reeling in more achievable goals.

If you choose achievable goals over wishful thinking, you can always work your way up. If you choose wishful thinking over achievable goals, you allow your ego to interfere. And this is never a good idea.

## Dreams of Fish on a Waning Crescent Moon

**KEY THOUGHT:** Optimism will always attract
more of what you require than pessimism

As the light of the sun recedes from the lunar surface, the shadow of the dark side of the moon merges with the infinite bleakness of space. The shadow and the space appear the same but are vastly different. Similarly, the shadow of lost opportunity can sometimes be confused with the bleakness of *no* opportunities and deflate you more than you should allow it to.

There are few things more eerie than the ocean depths; dark and silent, with only the most savage lurking in the abyss. Yet one cunning species, the angler fish, uses light to lure its prey. While it seems unlikely that anything placing any kind of value on vision could survive at this depth, the angler fish does thrive on the light and hope it radiates.

While you should probably not aspire to the false promises of the angler fish, Ishtar is reminding you that, no matter how bleak your emotional depths may seem, light and optimism will always attract more of what you desire than pessimism.

# Flying and Planes

When considering the meaning or interpretation of a dream, always keep in mind that Ishtar has no interest in vain flattery; she doesn't tell you what you want to hear. She tells you what you need to know so you can act on her guidance in your journey toward your best life.

Dreams of flight, whether this is jet-powered or self-propelled, relate to your subconscious or spiritual desires to become liberated, not a home video of real-time achievements.

Flight is, at its core, an escape to freedom from limiting forces. Whether from a geographic location, a lack of creative or spiritual inspiration, the weight of responsibility at work or in toxic relationships, there are many things that may be weighing you down that flight would free you from.

These flight dreams are no different from any other category with its many variants: powered or self-levitating, piloting or as a passenger, floating, above the clouds, or taking a bird's eye view of the landscape, each variant has its nuanced differences but share the general message: you long for freedom.

It is your job to work out what that means to you specifically, and also how the lunar phases colour the interpretation.

## Dreams of Flying and Planes on a New Moon

**KEY THOUGHT:** From what do you wish to take flight?

There is a nice symmetry with dreams of flying on the new moon. Now is a time of new beginnings, fresh starts, new ideas and clean slates. Poetically, this feeling of unbridled *creative* freedom fits well with dreams of flying, revealing deep yearning for unbridled *spiritual* freedom.

In your dream of flying, gravity is the oppressor. You can learn more if you examine what you are seeking, who is flying or if you are falling, and interpret these as desires. For example, if you see a spectacular bird's eye view, what you desire is perspective. What is oppressing perspective in your waking life?

Likewise, if you are falling in your dream, you lack support. You *desire* to be rid of responsibilities: free falling.

When you dream of flying on the new moon, the message from Ishtar is that you desire freedom from an oppressive situation. Now, it is up to you to identify what you wish to take flight from.

## Dreams of Flying and Planes on a Waxing Crescent Moon

**KEY THOUGHT:** Remove the things that prevent you from feeling uplifted

The waxing crescent moon is an exciting time to start acting on your passions. With the light of the sun creeping around the moon, illuminating its edge and pushing back shadows of doubt, its form is now implied if not fulfilled.

Similarly with life projects, many ideas may not feel satisfying until they are completed. Yet, enjoying the process of their completion is the key to happiness, not the completion itself.

When interpreting dreams of flying, look at your subconscious desire to escape the bindings of your everyday routines and see the world differently. You desire to be lifted up – uplifted, and just as you desire it, you also deserve it.

When Royal Air Force pilots are ready to taxi their plane to prepare for take-off, their direction to the ground crew is "Chocks away". Chocks are triangular blocks placed in front of and behind a plane's wheels to preventing it from rolling. "Chocks away" is your cue to remove them so you can move forward, escape the pull of gravity and uplift your spirit.

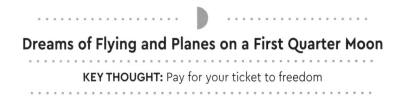

# Dreams of Flying and Planes on a First Quarter Moon

**KEY THOUGHT:** Pay for your ticket to freedom

Being earthbound is two-dimensional compared to the added options of up and down of flying. Dating back to the earliest prehistoric times, humans have desired the ability to fly. Whether to escape predators, feel weightless or just to feel free, the reasons are less important than the grand unifying longing humans have for flight. It is extraordinary to think that, in just 65 years, humans went from a pedestrian species to an interplanetary one.

Getting Neil Armstrong to the moon required, above all else, the strong arm of conviction: the will to fly. And this is what dreams on the first quarter moon call out for.

But conviction in what?

Dreams of flying expose a deep yearning for freedom or escape. These forces that tether you in real life may be gravitational, but this is probably not what Ishtar is concerned about. She has a different view of the world.

Restrictive finances, micro-managing bosses, shyness and responsibilities can pin you down or crush your spirit. If you are ever to break the bonds that repress you, you must first acquire the will to do it. You must commit to the effort before you make it and pay for the ticket to freedom before you board.

## Dreams of Flying and Planes
## on a Waxing Gibbous Moon

**KEY THOUGHT:** Keep your spiritual GPS switched on

There have been many times when, while sitting on a plane for endless hours, I have stared at the real-time map of where the plane is in relation to the earth. When I feel the plane tilt for a few seconds before it levels off again, I wonder what made the pilot turn then rather than later or earlier. Then I wonder how far off course the plane would be in four hours if it didn't make that subtle tweak to its direction.

Dreams of flying on the waxing gibbous moon are a calling from Ishtar to make you aware that you desire freedom and that while you are well on your way, minor tweaks in your pursuits now could make profound differences in where you land.

Just because you have taken flight, you would be wise to keep your spiritual GPS switched on.

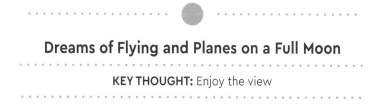

## Dreams of Flying and Planes on a Full Moon

**KEY THOUGHT:** Enjoy the view

There is a palpable shift in energy inside a plane once it has reached its cruising altitude. The engines relax, the seatbelt sign goes off, people start milling around, and, of course, the drinks trolley starts its slow crawl to the cramped middle seat in row 40. There is more of a sense of "arrival" – plus, it is a spectacular view.

Similarly, as the moon becomes fully illuminated and full, it communicates power and energy. Not only does it look spectacular, it also lights the night – a view of unique beauty.

Wherever you are in life, whatever stresses and turbulence you experience, whatever fears you have, there are times when you must put these aside and simply enjoy the view of your life.

## Dreams of Flying and Planes on a Waning Gibbous Moon

**KEY THOUGHT:** Take responsibility for how grounded you are

What goes up must come down, and what waxes full will soon begin to wane.

Dreams of flying on the waning gibbous moon are messages from Ishtar that while you desire freedom from whatever holds you down, you must understand that freedom comes with its own set of responsibilities.

In the same way that the opposite of "love" isn't "hate" but is "indifference", the opposite of being controlled isn't a complete lack of control; it is taking control.

If there is any facet of your life where you feel you have given up control or that it has been taken from you, it would be worth a moment of your time to ask yourself if that has in any way compromised your spiritual wellbeing.

This could suggest major factors such as relationships or work, but Ishtar may be talking about more subtle personal control issues. From periodically cutting out alcohol to doing your own laundry, making dinner rather than ordering it in, to reclaiming ownership of your health and fitness, there are many ways you can take responsibility for how grounded you are.

## Dreams of Flying and Planes on a Third Quarter Moon

**KEY THOUGHT:** Expect turbulence, but don't let that stop you

Just as reaching cruising altitude feels like the most relaxing moment of any flight, preparing for the final approach seems the busiest. Banking left and right, encountering turbulence, and the clunks and whines of the landing gear and the wing flaps all convey that, upfront, there is a lot going on.

Dreams of flying at any time project onto your consciousness your deep desire for greater freedom in life. Breaking free is incredibly liberating, yet only half the battle. Talking control so you can land safely – taking responsibility for and ownership of your choices – can often be met with its own turbulence, and not just by others. You can often be your own judge and jury on matters of personal choices.

As you journey through life, you should expect these bumps, rattles, doubts and crosswinds. As long as you have lowered the landing gear, thought through your actions and spoken with air traffic control, and communicated clearly with those you love about your intentions, you can trust that the wings of your ambition and the air you breathe will do the rest.

You can expect turbulence, but that shouldn't deter you.

## Dreams of Flying and Planes on a Waning Crescent Moon

**KEY THOUGHT:** Breathe in the new, exhale the old

When I travel by air, I look forward to landing. However, I don't get that feeling of "arriving" until I have gone through passport control and customs, collected luggage and stepped out into the craziness of the taxi ranks, and breathed the air of my new emotional space.

Taking care of the finishing touches of any escape can make all the difference to the experience of being in a new location, geographically and spiritually. Dreams of flying on a waning crescent moon are messages sent to remind you that, as much as your psyche may wish for liberation from its confines, and as much work as you may have put into growing emotionally to take more responsibility, there are always details to attend to before you can call it your home.

By breathing in the new and exhaling the old, you can settle into any situation with serenity and a feeling of adventure.

# Guns and Being Shot

Guns strike at the heart of our instinct for self-preservation: When a gun is pulled, nothing else matters. Regardless of our status, wealth or influence, if we are held at gunpoint, we are powerless. From pop culture to street violence, guns are everywhere. And what is worse, guns are handheld, concealed, covert and sly – they are also invisible. No matter the circumstance, anyone who is defenceless but then pulls a concealed gun turns the tables in an instant.

When you turn from the waking world to the dream world, your perspective must change. You must seek to understand how the imprint of guns influences your subconscious.

In dreams, guns represent power and the abuse of it, and gunshots in your dreams represent victimization. When you analyze Ishtar's messages, it is important to focus on the emotions, not the subjects. In many cases, the wielder of the gun may look like a stranger but represent yourself, showing that you are being too hard on yourself, punishing yourself or shooting yourself in the foot in acts of self-sabotage.

The bottom line is that guns in dreams equate to feelings of power, fear, defence, anger and revenge. As with all dreams, Ishtar isn't here to instill fear, but to advise.

You have *one shot* at life, and when you dream of guns, Ishtar is saying that the power is yours to ensure it is your *best* shot. But you should also know that this power is only ever *offered* to you, never *given*; it is for you to take.

While we are here, I would like to share a story I wrote for my children a few years ago that feels like it should live in this chapter. I hope you enjoy it and see the relevance.

# SHOOTING STARS

*Once upon a time, there lived a boy who loved shooting guns.*

*"I never want to do anything else," he would say.*

*In the morning, he shot at stones that lay on the ground. And he hit many. In the afternoon, he raised his sights and shot at flowers that grew in the meadows. And he hit many. And in the evening, he raised his sights and shot at leaves that swayed high in the trees. And he hit many.*

*When darkness fell, and he could see no more, he began to walk home. Just as he reached his gate, he raised his sights one last time and saw the moon. This was surely the most magnificent of all targets, so he began to shoot at the moon. And he hit it many times.*

*"Why are you shooting at me?" the moon protested.*

*"Because you are the brightest and most magnificent of all things in the night sky," he answered.*

*"I am an easy target," the moon admitted. "But I am also the wrong*

*target. You would be better served aiming for the stars."*

*"But they are so small and so distant," the boy complained.*

*"Exactly," replied the moon.*

*And so, the boy aimed at the stars. And he missed many times. The next night he tried again. And again, he missed many times. He shot at Orion's Belt and Cassiopeia, Vega and Sirius. And he always missed. He even shot at shooting stars. Night after night, week after week, and year after year, he aimed at the stars through his viewfinder. But he never ever hit a star.*

*Then there came a night, many years later, when the moon saw the boy, now fully grown, staring at the night sky.*

*"Why are you not shooting at stars?" asked the moon. "Did you give up your guns?"*

*"Oh no," replied the man. "I became a champion marksman."*

*"Is this what you do for a living?" asked the moon.*

*"No," replied the man. "I am an astronomer. Once I set my sights on the sky and saw its infinite beauty, I never wanted to be anything else."*

*"Very good," said the moon. "You looked up. You aimed high. You set your sights on noble goals and saw beauty. And you never gave up. Very good, indeed."*

## Dreams of Guns and Being Shot on a New Moon

**KEY THOUGHT:** Lay down your arms and retain your power

Dreams of guns are expressions of fear and powerlessness, and dreams on the new moon are an open invitation to explore new ideas. Ignorance may or may not be bliss. But entering new situations with a childlike enthusiasm and avoiding gossip, tactical relationships and pandering to egos can keep you far from the fray.

And remember, if you live by the sword (or gun, gossip or bad-mouthing), you will fall victim to the same. In any new situation, lay down your arms and retain your power.

## Dreams of Guns and Being Shot on a Waxing Crescent Moon

**KEY THOUGHT:** Remain flexible in the roles you play in life

If the new moon is the canvas and the full moon the masterpiece, the waxing crescent moon represents the first bold brush strokes. It is the phase that begins to put plans into action. Dreams of guns are all about power. As you travel through different phases of a project, relationship and life, your roles may feel more or less powerful. But it doesn't need to feel that way. The waxing crescent moon is a symbol of life and death and positive action. Now is the time to ramp up your efforts.

While you may have been developing ideas for a while, the first step, though uncreative in itself, speaks loudly to your community. The architect hands over his plans before the first foundation is dug, your destination is defined before you leave your front door, and the plan of attack is signed off before the first bullet is fired. Yet while the architect, trip planner and general each hand over their power as soon as their work is done, it is handed to the bricklayer, driver and rifleman. This isn't a downgrade; this is the natural process of an evolving plan.

As you begin and develop any endeavour, if you can remain flexible throughout the project, you can keep hold of your power, purpose, pride and, ultimately, your happiness.

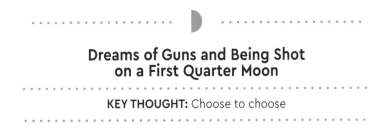

## Dreams of Guns and Being Shot on a First Quarter Moon

**KEY THOUGHT:** Choose to choose

The first quarter moon is also known as the half moon. From our perspective, it is half lit and half in shadow. Whether we regard this as positive or negative is, again, a matter of perspective.

If in your dream you were shot and survived, you can *choose* to see the dream as positive. If you die in your dream, you can *choose* to see it as the death of the cynic in you. You can *choose* a positive outlook. It is then up to you to pull the trigger.

Pulling the trigger is a well-known and widely used phrase that represents making a critical decision to go. Dreams of guns on the first quarter moon are Ishtar's way of saying you must pull the trigger or walk away. In short, it is decision time.

Many inspirational speakers and business advisers talk about the skills required in leadership. At the top of the list is confidence in making decisions. You may have tried to be democratic when choosing, say, a restaurant to eat in. How often do you remain unsure until someone says, "That's it, enough of this, let's go to this place"? The choice may or may not have been the best, but it matters less if no other choice was made.

Similarly, a skiing friend once asked me, "If you are skiing and are heading toward a tree, what should you do?" The answer is, of course, anything. Any turn will be better than hitting the tree.

Dreams of guns on the first quarter moon are about power; keeping it and not surrendering it. It is about staying on track by choice. Power is most clearly expressed when you make decisions, and most clearly surrendered when you allow others to choose for you.

Choose to choose.

## Dreams of Guns and Being Shot on a Waxing Gibbous Moon

**KEY THOUGHT:** Are you aiming at the right things in life?

When you dream of guns on the waxing gibbous moon, you dream of power and the refined actions you need to take to maintain your voice.

Guns have an unnatural hold on psyches, and, of course, they are ubiquitous in contemporary media and the news. As with any refined skill, the master craftsman should be respected, whether they are a fisherman, musician or, in this case, marksman. When watching a sharpshooter, notice how long he takes to set his sights, calibrating and fine-tuning his view so that, when he does finally pull the trigger, he will achieve his goal.

With dreams of guns on the waxing gibbous moon, you are receiving messages from Ishtar that you must focus, set your sights and calibrate your vision of your goals.

Now is the time to ask yourself if you are aiming at the right things in life.

# Dreams of Guns and Being Shot on a Full Moon

**KEY THOUGHT:** Don't ask "Can I?", ask "*Will* I?"

Dreams on the full moon speak to completion and the energy of fulfillment, the climax, the final achievement. With most things that need effort to achieve them, there is usually an accompanying feeling of anticlimax. Dreams of guns pertain to feelings of power, so when you experience a dream about guns on the full moon, Ishtar is prompting you to consider where you may be experiencing conflicting feelings of power and powerlessness – climax and anticlimax – and how you can reconcile this inner conflict.

The moment a climber reaches the mountaintop, the primary driver that got him there – the desire to ascend – is no longer relevant. The mantra of "I must climb higher and work harder to achieve my goal" was obsessive, yet upon the zenith the feeling of achievement may last for only a fleeting moment before it is replaced with "So, what's next?" The power he evoked to fuel his drive is instantly drained: climax and anticlimax.

If you were to meet this climber, perhaps you would be more interested in his *ability to achieve* than the *achievement itself*. If he can summon the will to "climb higher and work harder" to get to this goal, maybe he could apply that will to anything. His *will* is the more exciting part of his achievement. In fact, in my opinion, his will *is* his achievement.

Think of his *will* as his power.

Don't ask "Can I?", ask "*Will* I?"

## Dreams of Guns and Being Shot on a Waning Gibbous Moon

**KEY THOUGHT:** Identify your fields of freedom

The waxing gibbous moon is a time when shadows begin to creep over the moon's surface, diminishing its power. Since dreams about guns pertain to power and fear, there is a clear correlation between the two that speaks to the fear of losing our power in our waking life.

When you dream of guns on the waning gibbous – no matter who is holding the gun and who (if anyone) gets shot – you receive messages from Ishtar that you need to be aware of the little ways you surrender power and ask yourself why you do this.

Surrendering control can take many forms. From job-related power struggles to interpersonal battles of will to personal struggles of will_power_, there are a million tiny ways you can surrender power. And when I say power, I also mean self-esteem and happiness. Yet it doesn't have to be this way.

When Marc Gonsalves was taken hostage in the jungles of South America, he was chained to a tree for five years. With a broken piece of a machete, he carved chess pieces, and on a piece of cardboard he drew a chess board on which he and the other hostages played. For five years, chess immersed their minds and allowed their thoughts to be free and their decisions to be their own, unchained. After their release, they touted this freedom as a lifesaver.

Victor Frankl tells a similar story of mental freedom. Frankl went from Auschwitz prisoner to high-profile Nuremberg journalist to author of the profound _Man's Search for Meaning_, all within twelve months. He argues in his book that happiness is a choice, no matter one's circumstances.

Power is a frame of mind, and Ishtar knows it. Dreams of guns on the waning gibbous moon are about framing your situation in an empowering way. After all, the waning gibbous moon is still mostly bright.

No matter your circumstances, you should identify your fields of freedom because you will be your happiest there.

## Dreams of Guns and Being Shot on a Third Quarter Moon

**KEY THOUGHT:** Focus on what you see, not what you fear

The third quarter moon is a tense time in the lunar calendar, because it indicates that winter is coming with its shadow in ascent and light in decline.

Dreams of guns are visions from your subconscious mind that relate to power and fear. No matter the circumstances within the dream, the key message Ishtar is sending in dreams of guns on the third quarter moon is that while there may be things you can't overpower, there are things *within* your power that can protect you from harm. Any sports coach will tell you that while games are won in offence, seasons are won in defence.

Your power may not have led to you being let go from your place of work, but it is in your power to think of the forced transition as something you will look back on as being pivotal in your journey to more enjoyable and suitable work. Your power may not lead your partner to betray you, but it is in your power to own at least some of the responsibility for allowing the relationship to drift; reflect on your role and grow from the experience. While some aspects of your health may not be in your power to fix, that doesn't mean you should surrender, squander or neglect the power you *do* have over your wellbeing.

You don't "see" shadows; you only see *light*. Shadows are simply the lack of light. Don't focus on what you fear but on what you *see*.

## Dreams of Guns and Being Shot on a Waning Crescent Moon

**KEY THOUGHT:** There is more power in flexibility than in flexing

Dreams on the waning crescent moon are Ishtar's way of prompting you to seek resolution in your waking life. Dreams of guns are Ishtar's way of prompting you to consider the various forms of power (or powerlessness), fear and anger you may be experiencing.

Finding the peace of mind to roll with the punches is easier said than done. Many sayings from many eras and civilizations come to mind to support this idea. One of my favorites is Chinese: "The tree that does not sway in the wind will snap."

In the context of dreams of guns on the waning crescent moon, we can expand this proverb to say that, as a result, the tree that does sway will harbour no resentment toward the wind. Why would it? Furthermore, it may even have used the wind to disperse its seeds far and wide.

How different the experiences of these two trees are. How powerful must the inflexible tree have felt before the wind, and how prosperous the flexible one became after the storm.

There is more power in flexibility than in flexing; if flexing is ego, flexibility is soul. And Ishtar is urging you to see that seeking resolution, releasing resentment and bending with the wind will not only protect you from breaking but will also sow seeds of kindness far and wide.

# Hair

Hair! Can't live with it; can't live without it. It is extraordinary how much time people spend managing their hair. Cutting, growing, colouring, bleaching, curling, straightening, washing, drying – the list is endless.

And for what? To express themselves, conform to social standards, or rebel *against* them. There are some correlations between certain hairstyles and specific life choices or music preferences. With the possible exception of neglect, any style is a statement.

Gaining control over our hair isn't always possible, yet if our hair looks good we feel better, interact socially, impress professionally and can give a good impression in other forms of activity. Only the most confident people wouldn't check their appearance before an important meeting. Anxiety around getting hair under control is intimately connected to social acceptance: classic dream material.

## Dreams of Hair on a New Moon

**KEY THOUGHT:** Mirror, mirror, on the wall, are you being fair to yourself?

Few things in life more powerfully affect someone's mood than their own messy, unruly hair or a sleek new haircut. The power contained in the hairstylist's scissors is hard to quantify on an emotional level.

Dreams of hair on the new moon are a calling from Ishtar that there are things within your control that you can do for yourself to help lift your mood and self-esteem.

The different types of hair dreams are too numerous to address individually, but hair in a dream is generally your opinion of your waking-life state of affairs. Too messy? Tangled? Lacking in shine and sex appeal? Falling out? Greying? Each condition provokes an emotional response, and that response within the dream provides the key to the dream interpretation.

If in the dream you are getting your hair done or dyeing it, you can interpret this as dissatisfaction with certain aspects of your life. Since there is little you can do about your natural hair colour, you may want to seek ways to work on patience and acceptance. Or, if in the dream you are detangling a friend's hair and are enjoying the time chatting, this may suggest that you are too easily distracted from self-care as you work to fix other people's problems.

Dreaming of hair on the new moon allows you to peep into your subconscious and consider if you are taking care of your priorities appropriately. It gives you a chance to look into the mirror and ask if you are being fair to yourself.

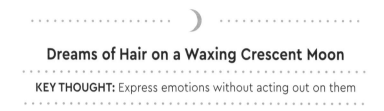

## Dreams of Hair on a Waxing Crescent Moon

**KEY THOUGHT:** Express emotions without acting out on them

The waxing crescent moon is a time when, astronomically and spiritually, you start to put plans into action. These are things that have remained purely conceptual, safely out of the reach of criticism, expense or failure, but are now ready to be realized. This is an exciting and possibly nervewracking moment for you to take a step forward.

As with any step forward, the *step* is only half the decision, and what constitutes "forward" is the other half: direction is key.

Dreams of hair are dreams of self image. How you imagine *others* see you may be different from how you see yourself; the former is social grooming and the latter is vanity. Dreams of hair on the waxing crescent moon are Ishtar's way of keeping you honest.

Efforts made focusing on social grooming while stopping short of vanity won't be . . . well . . . in vain. Of course, Ishtar isn't referring to hair; she is referring to outlook and emotional presentation. Being able to express emotions without acting out on them is a good start.

. . . . . . . . . . . . . . . . . . . . . ◗ . . . . . . . . . . . . . . . . . . .

## Dreams of Hair on a First Quarter Moon

. . . . . . . . . . . . . . . . . . . . . . . . . . . . . . . . . . . . . . . . . . .

**KEY THOUGHT:** Nurture traits that better suit your ideal self-image

. . . . . . . . . . . . . . . . . . . . . . . . . . . . . . . . . . . . . . . . . . .

Sometimes, indecision is the worst decision, and sometimes a bad decision is better than avoiding the issue. Dreams of hair on the first quarter call you to take the leap, make the decision and radically change how you present yourself. At the very least, no one will notice, yet you will reduce your internal stress. At best, others will love the change. Making a conscious decision about how you want to feel and present to others can be a healthy exercise in identifying what doesn't work and trying something new.

Just as you may flick through magazines and see hair you love, dreams of hair reflect how you want to change on a more emotional level. Whether this is finances, social situations or work, your dreams can inspire you in many ways. If you are capable of realization, you can adopt and nurture the traits that better suit your ideal emotional self-image.

## Dreams of Hair on a Waxing Gibbous Moon

. . . . . . . . . . . . . . . . . . . . . . . . . . . . . . . . . . . . . . . . . . .

**KEY THOUGHT:** Detangling life knots will add bounce
to your stride and shine to your smile

. . . . . . . . . . . . . . . . . . . . . . . . . . . . . . . . . . . . . . . . . . .

Dreams of hair on the waxing gibbous moon are messages from Ishtar that, while there may be messy, tangled and unkempt situations in your life, the right conditioner – or the right hat – can easily fix the problem.

Conditioner means an honest conversation about how you are feeling to detangle a complex relationship or taking a second, part-time job to clean up a few messy debts.

Detangling life knots will add bounce to your stride and shine to your smile.

## Dreams of Hair on a Full Moon

**KEY THOUGHT:** Make the most of what you have

Many people have struggled with the kind of hair they have. Ironically, people whose hair you may envy are likely to struggle just as you do. Too curly, no personality, too fine, too thick . . . the complaints about hair are almost as varied as people are. Accepting what your hair _is_ and letting go of what it is _not_ is the first step to making the most of what you have.

Dreams of hair on the full moon are Ishtar's way of bringing into focus your awareness of your self-identity and accepting what you can't change. The serenity prayer is classic and certainly apt. When you dream of hair, you dream of controlling the adversity you are dealt. Dry hair or an emotionally distant mother, thinning ponytail or redundancies at work, there are things you just have to accept.

Yet having the strength to change the things you can affect – lowering expectations, seeking new employment – is the message you are being sent.

Your hair is what you are given; your style is what you do with it. You must make the most of what you have.

## Dreams of Hair on a Waning Gibbous Moon

**KEY THOUGHT:** Trimming off the split ends of life will improve your spiritual condition

Hairdressers often say that by cutting their client's hair, they transform their life. While this may sound overly dramatic, they have a point. Only they can know the number of times a week a client may come into their salon down on themselves after a recent breakup, and only they can see that client transformed into a re-energized, confident person as they leave: transformed.

Sprucing up your look, job, wardrobe or even relationships can do wonders for your perspective. This may sound shallow, and if you were to talk about adding material things to your collection, it may be. But there are ways to improve your outlook by removing as well.

Dreams of hair on the waning gibbous moon are messages from Ishtar that you may benefit from a trim. From split ends to a radical cut, trimming from your life can be a game changer. Digital detoxing – signing off social media for a month – is a trim. Separating from an abusive relationship is a radical cut. Meatless Mondays, no wine on weekdays for a month or cycling to work are all ways to simplify. Ishtar is urging you to consider what you can trim from your life.

Trimming off your split ends of life will improve your spiritual condition.

## Dreams of Hair on a Third Quarter Moon

**KEY THOUGHT:** Cut off life's tangles. You will look better

How many people have had a tangle in their hair that was so severe that no amount of conditioning and combing could get rid of the mess? Life can be a little like that: where some areas of life feel silky smooth, others may feel like an inextricable and complex web of relationships, finances or expectations.

What do you tend to do in these situations? Dreams of hair on the third quarter moon are Ishtar's way of telling you that it is time to cut off the tangles that pull painfully, make you look foolish or have you caught up in someone else's struggle.

Pulling at these entanglements may cause additional pain, but consulting with others, especially experts in these matters, is the best way of separating yourself from uncomfortable situations with ease and grace. If you are lucky, you may even come out looking good.

It doesn't matter what you do in life or how you look. What matters is that you take care of yourself, keep your spirits tangle-free and in good condition, and remain open to looking within yourself and listening to the lessons life teaches you.

## Dreams of Hair on a Waning Crescent Moon

**KEY THOUGHT:** Tend to your inner beauty as diligently as you tend to your outer beauty

Many women and some men were told when they were young that they were to brush their hair 100 times daily to keep it from getting messy. While we can't know if a one-remedy-fits-all really does fit all, we take its point.

By taking regular care of your affairs, you can avoid messes. A spiritual practice is a daily routine to stop tiny knots from becoming big ones. The warning crescent moon precedes the new moon, and dreams of hair during this moon cycle urge you to reflect on the small problems in your life and start to unravel clear intentions. Creating your own intentions and removing the small knots is best done when the moon is dark.

Dreams of hair on the waning crescent moon are messages from Ishtar that you should tend to your inner beauty as frequently and diligently as you tend to your outer beauty.

Look up at the moon. The waning crescent moon reminds you that while the visible crescent is bright, the moon is much more than just what you see. You are *pulled* by what you *feel*. Yoga, meditation, a fitness regime and a healthy diet are all healthy practices that tend to your inner beauty. We don't need to do these things 100 times a day: a few times a week would be plenty.

# Hotels and Holidays

Luxury or budget, business or pleasure, with company or alone, exotic resort or roadside motel, the mission of any type of hotel is the same: to cater to the needs of temporary guests.

Hotels are designed for people on the move, between points, away from home. Relationships with hotels, even with preferred ones, have no long-term commitment. This is a business relationship – they cater to your needs on a temporary basis, for a fee. And the price is proportional to the level of service provided.

Dreams are about the *implied relationships* rather than what they *appear* to be about, and hotel dreams are no exception. This chapter is about the price you pay for accommodation while away from home.

Despite your desire for stability, life doesn't always offer it, and certainly never promises it. You can do your best to create stability, and that safe place is what you may call home, distinct from hotels. Transitions, temporary states of mind, uncommitted or temporary emotional relationships and shifts in perspective are all up for interpretation when you dream of hotels.

## Dreams of Hotels and Holidays on a New Moon

**KEY THOUGHT:** Consider your next move with special care

When you dream, repressed impulses are expressed in your conscious mind. These can be desires or fears and, if interpreted correctly, can offer deep personal insight, self-awareness, and ultimately greater peace of mind that you are on the right path.

It is particularly interesting when you dream of hotels that speak of a desire for or fear for transition, turning off the path you are on. Add to that the creative energy of the new moon – with its mystery, openness to ideas and undefined form – and you have a volatile and exciting message of dissatisfaction with the status quo and a desire for spontaneity and escape.

When you dream of hotels, you should check that you are not being reckless or irresponsible. Desiring escape from the mundane is perfectly natural. You must be sure you have booked your room before you leave home and consider your next move with special care.

## Dreams of Hotels and Holidays on a Waxing Crescent Moon

**KEY THOUGHT:** Keep in touch with your personal anchors

Now that the moon is in its waxing crescent phase, its form is beginning to radiate truth and substance in a tide of light that pushes back doubt. You are entering a time when ideas start to take shape. In your waking life, you may have to spin many plates. Work, partners, creativity, finances, social life and intellectual appetite all need attention, and at any given time, some may require more than others.

When you dream on the waxing crescent moon, you should look at what you have neglected and pay a visit to that aspect of your psyche.

Dreams of hotels represent a feeling of desire for a temporary, casual affair with this part of your life. Perhaps it is a short escape from your more stable and possibly uninspiring emotional home – or maybe the neglect of the household budget has left you feeling distant from the security of knowing your financial situation.

Being away from home can be unsettling, no matter how good you are made to feel in the moment. Keeping in touch with personal anchors – friends, family, work, financial reality or any other grounding activity or relationship – can make all the difference between feeling homesick and enjoying the break.

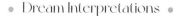

## Dreams of Hotels and Holidays on a First Quarter Moon

**KEY THOUGHT:** Have a plan in your back pocket for what's next

Hotels, by design, offer a temporary stay, from when you check in to when you check out. Before and after these dates are the rest of your life; between them lives a community of comers and goers.

It isn't often that you check in to a transitional situation without any awareness of your check-out date, at least not in the real world, but Ishtar has access to your subconscious itinerary. She can see the plan and will speak up if the cost of indecision looks like it may bankrupt your emotional bank account. Dreams in the first quarter moon are all about making decisions.

You can only tread water and live off room service for so long. If you know an element of your life is temporary – and let's face it, most elements are – you should celebrate that fact, enjoy the break, accept the check-out date when it arrives, and have a plan in your back pocket for what happens after that.

## Dreams of Hotels and Holidays on a Waxing Gibbous Moon

**KEY THOUGHT:** Tend to the details of the transient elements of your life

Hotels are superficially and experientially very different when it comes to luxury, but what they have in common is that they attend to your needs. On the lower end of the spectrum, the service is basic: security, shelter and rest. The further up the spectrum, the finer the attention to detail you experience.

When you dream of hotels on the waxing gibbous moon, Ishtar is bringing your awareness to areas in your life that retain a sense of instability, transience and insecurity. As you journey through life, you are inevitably in flux in at least some area of your life: perhaps you are in a stable relationship but "between jobs"; maybe you are in a stable job but have to move apartments. There is always something.

Dreams of hotels on the waxing gibbous moon are Ishtar's way of ensuring you tend to the details of the transient elements of your life; these are as much a part of your journey as the stable parts.

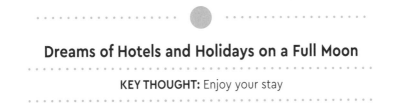

## Dreams of Hotels and Holidays on a Full Moon

**KEY THOUGHT:** Enjoy your stay

Powerful energy during the full moon reveals the big picture in bright light. The full moon is honest and unflinching, illuminating more brightly than at any other time. This is the moment you have been waiting for.

Yet as surely as the full moon arrives, you know its departure is guaranteed. It is as temporary as it is magnificent, and as magnificent as it is temporary.

With very few exceptions (such as family and select lifelong friends), everything you experience in life is temporary. If you want to be existential about it, you could argue life itself is temporary, but this is Ishtar's world and she is dedicated to your terrestrial wellbeing. Dreams of hotels on the full moon are her way of opening your eyes to the reality (and cost) of the temporary stops you make in your life journey.

When you accept that any job, lover, home, passion, illness, wellness, youth and attitude will (most likely) be temporary – as will those of others in your life – you can regard them honestly, file them appropriately, rely on them conditionally, and be okay when things change.

In other words: you should make every effort to enjoy your stay.

## Dreams of Hotels and Holidays
## on a Waning Gibbous Moon

**KEY THOUGHT:** Leave your home when you debug it

Dreams of hotels on the waning gibbous moon are a sign from Ishtar that you may need to stay in a temporary situation – even if it is unpleasant – as you make changes in your life to adjust to new shadows.

If you think about why you haven't done something you think you long for, or stay in an unhealthy situation that makes you unhappy, you may believe that transitioning would cause too much drama for it to be worthwhile. Stepping back from an unhealthy emotional relationship, seeking new employment, going to the gym or saving up for a new car are all temporary discomforts for the greater good.

If you can positively frame any form of temporary limbo as a shelter from the storm whenever you have to debug an aspect of your life, you will be more able to manage the inconvenience with gratitude.

## Dreams of Hotels and Holidays
## on a Third Quarter Moon

**KEY THOUGHT:** It is time to depart from dependency

Travel can be exciting, addictive, perpetually unsettling and often uncomfortable. One thing it is *not* is mundane. Even the most hardened business travellers are on constant alert. Yet when you are in a state of transition, you may sometimes become used to the room service. If budget weren't an issue, many people would prefer to be catered for rather than take care of their domestic responsibilities.

Dreams of hotels on the third quarter moon speak to your limbo and desire for stability, recognizing that while room service (in other words, being supported) is convenient, your self-esteem will have to pick up the tab eventually. Plus, it is never as good as home cooking. Your dream on the third quarter moon is a call for Ishtar to start looking at your check-out date.

Whatever life has dealt you, whatever limbo you feel trapped in, you know deep down that taking responsibility for ending your reliance on other people, and returning to the stability and self-esteem that independence gives you, is the home you need to return to.

It is time to depart from dependency.

## Dreams of Hotels and Holidays on a Waning Crescent Moon

**KEY THOUGHT:** Wherever you go, know where home is

As incredible as any holiday could be – or any other form of escape for that matter, such as a road trip, an extramarital affair or training for a marathon – returning home is a uniquely beautiful feeling.

Home can be interpreted in many ways, and can be a state of mind. Dreams of hotels on the waning crescent moon are about areas in your life that fill you with a sense of transience. Whether luxurious or seedy, temporary stays, casual relationships and novelty excitement are exactly that; temporary, casual and just a novelty.

Wherever you go, you can enjoy your travels fully only if you know where home is.

# Houses and Homes

Imagine you are asked to picture yourself as a house, with each room of that house representing an aspect of your personality, and then you are told to draw it in a doll's house style, with its front wall missing, offering complete visibility into each room. What would your self-portrait look like?

Now imagine you are a psychologist and have been asked to analyze your drawing. What would you think? What might the attic represent? The kitchen? The bedroom? The basement? What would it mean if the house was empty? What if the gardens were gorgeous while the inside was chaotic and neglected? What if the house was empty while the basement was crowded? What if the bedroom was decorated, but the kitchen wasn't?

The house in your imagination can't just represent components of your present-day waking life; it can also represent your past and future. From the nursery to the playroom, the bedroom to the kitchen, the study to the garden, each room can relate to phases of your life.

Dreams of houses are, as Freud once said, dreams of "thy self". Framed in the above way – a container for various compartments of self-image – you may see what is made public and what is kept secret, where your priorities lie, whether you care to nourish yourself and if you care for the exterior differently than the interior.

Dreams of houses are selfies of esteem, pride, awareness, what you hide in the attic, and show to which rooms you leave doors wide open.

There is perhaps no dream category that so clearly reveals itself; if not what you are *now*, then what Ishtar believes you *desire to be*.

# Dreams of Houses and Homes on a New Moon

**KEY THOUGHT:** Renovate your life

Dreams on the new moon are desires painted on a blank canvas and should be interpreted as a prompt for you to think about change. These are not a call to action, but can provide insight for a review without the energy required to commit.

Specifically for dreams of houses on the new moon, the analogy can be extended as a fixer-upper that you are thinking of buying. If you were to walk around a potential purchase, what questions would you ask yourself, and how can you interpret Ishtar's message?

Do the kitchen and bathrooms need work? (Could you take better care of yourself?) Are the basement and attic filled with clutter and need to be emptied? (Do you carry too many secrets?) Are the bedroom windows open to lovely views? (Do you desire healthy intimate relationships?) Why are there no doors or locks? (Do you leave yourself vulnerable to having your feelings hurt?)

Dreams of houses on the new moon are a wonderful place to examine how you can renovate your life.

# Dreams of Houses and Homes on a Waxing Crescent Moon

**KEY THOUGHT:** Make some psychological home improvements

When thinking about the meaning of dreams of houses on the waxing crescent moon, it is helpful to divide and conquer: the *house* represents the condition of your self-image, and the *waxing moon* asks you to start rebuilding the parts that need work.

When taking a look at the house, think about its condition and connect various rooms to various components of your inner self. The kitchen provides nourishment; the bathroom allows self-care and disposal of matters that no longer serve you; the home office is where you are practical and productive, and so on. The analogies are straightforward.

Also think about where you were in the house during your dream, your emotional state and your frustrations. If you were struggling to unlock a bedroom door or were hiding in the basement, these may be Ishtar's prompts to be more open in your waking life about your desires or the need to find ways to escape being held captive by your own secrets.

Whatever the case may be, the waxing moon tells you it is time to take action and start making some psychological home improvements.

## Dreams of Houses and Homes on a First Quarter Moon

**KEY THOUGHT:** Don't dither at the threshold of opportunity

As with all dreams of houses, the house represents "you", and in many other lunar phases the rooms in this house in your dreams can be interpreted as rooms in your psyche. What is most interesting about dreams of houses on the first quarter moon is that your interpretation should shift its focus to the *doors* and *hallways* rather than the rooms.

Dreams on the first quarter moon are Ishtar's way of pushing you to be decisive. The areas you are being encouraged to access are analogous to the doors that are open in the house in your dream.

If you can easily access areas of your life that have the doors opened for you – such as a job offer, a friend who has set you up on a blind date, or a chance to engage in a healthy or artistic pursuit – recognize these opportunities as open invitations. At that point, you have two options: walk *through* or walk *past*.

What you shouldn't do is dither at the threshold of opportunity.

## Dreams of Houses and Homes on a Waxing Gibbous Moon

**KEY THOUGHT:** Spruce up your internal décor

Dreams of houses on the waxing gibbous moon are dreams of self-image, which Ishtar tells you requires a little TLC. The waxing gibbous moon is almost fully illuminated with only a crescent of shadow, doubt and creative opportunity remaining. You should be able to see in your dream a house that is almost perfect yet perhaps in need of a little care. You can take this insight and project it onto your own psyche.

Simple home improvements may include changing lightbulbs or applying a fresh coat of paint. It is incredible how a little effort can go a long way to improve the feel of a room, and the same applies to your psyche. A little more illumination (awareness) in an area of your life that has been dark, or a fresh way of looking at your strengths instead of your weaknesses, can infinitely improve how you feel about yourself. Think of these as "lightbulb moments": ideas to spruce up your internal décor.

## Dreams of Houses and Homes on a Full Moon

**KEY THOUGHT:** Allow your garden to grow as you, and only you, wish it to

The full moon is a time of full illumination and high energy. It is a moment of climax or, if your hopes aren't met, *anti*climax. At the cusp of the waning phase, the full moon is a bittersweet apex of enlightenment.

Dreams of houses are projections of the state of your affairs and desires. To dream of a house in disrepair is to see yourself in the same way, as is to dream of a house that is empty, cold, locked or festive.

Dreams of houses on the full moon are incredible opportunities for you to see an honest image of yourself and be at peace with it.

You may ask if dreaming of a house in disrepair is negative or if a pristine show house is a good thing. This is where you must remember that Ishtar never tells you what you want to hear or hurts you unnecessarily; she tells you what you need to know.

When you dream of an apparently messy house, you also dream of a carefree, bohemian or artistic spirit, unburdened by a compulsion to tidy up in the hopes of approval from the neighbours.

The point is that you are who you are, and you are to be proud of that. You make the bed you *wish* to lie in, or you *don't* make the bed because you prefer it that way. There are no rules with spiritual housekeeping other than to allow your garden to grow as you, and only you, wish it to.

## Dreams of Houses and Homes
## on a Waning Gibbous Moon

**KEY THOUGHT:** Maintain a good spiritual housekeeping routine

One of the frustrating things about housekeeping for some people is that it is never finished. Other people may see it as a process, like driving, requiring minor, regular adjustments to keep them on track – this is most apt when dreams of houses happen on the waning gibbous moon.

Like domestic housework, *spiritual* housework is a process of maintaining good spirits. Patching up damage when it is small and addressing the root cause requires less work than allowing the cause of the damage to create greater problems.

Dreams of houses on the waning gibbous moon are Ishtar's way of prompting you to keep a clean spiritual house. If this means regularly checking in, meditating on challenges and avoiding getting stuck in a rut, so be it. You can limit damage by taking an honest personal inventory through yoga, running, meditation or talking openly with trusted friends.

To live your best life, you must maintain a good spiritual housekeeping routine.

## Dreams of Houses and Homes on a Third Quarter Moon

**KEY THOUGHT:** Dump emotional clutter

When you dream of houses on the third quarter moon, you dream of your self-image in the form of a house with many psychic spaces, doors and connections. An interesting exercise would be to draw a line from the rooms in the house you dreamed of to your own psychic spaces: intellect, art, work, social, self-care, etc.

Are there cluttered rooms in your psyche that may benefit from purging the junk you have stored in them for years? By dumping emotional clutter – toxic friendships, debts, secrets, self-destructive habits, etc. – you can create space, open the windows and allow sunlight and a fresh breeze into your life.

## Dreams of Houses and Homes on a Waning Crescent Moon

**KEY THOUGHT:** Secure the healthy things in your life

When you dream of houses on the waning crescent moon, you dream of yourself at the end of the day. The house in your dream represents the various components of your personality, and the waning crescent is a call from Ishtar to wrap things up.

What do you do to end the night? You lock the doors, close the windows and the curtains and turn the power off. This is the message you should see when you dream of houses on the waning crescent moon.

Loose ends in your life could take many forms: a definitive end to a slow breakup, accepting a job offer, settling on a regular health plan, getting that aching tooth seen to, and so on.

By securing the healthy things in your home and your life, you can rest assured that you are living your best life.

# Money

One of the most important things to remember when interpreting your dreams is that the images and narratives during the unconscious state of sleep are projections of your subconscious, not opinions of your conscious. It is almost as if your dream self speaks a different language to your waking self. It certainly has a different set of values, trading in the emotional world not the material one. While it may use objects such as money as symbols, wealth symbolizes emotional wellbeing: abundance in energy, opportunity, confidence and creativity.

Dreams of money – including its scarcity, theft, debt or loans – are analogies for spiritual riches, the most important type of resource as far as Ishtar is concerned. Emotionally positive money dreams – in which, no matter the narrative, you are happy within the dream – can relate to new and plentiful opportunities, general contentment and security, creative energy and freedom. Conversely, emotionally negative money dreams could relate to limited opportunities, or at least the feeling of limits.

Money in its physical form is a challenge for everyone. Few people complain about having too much, and wealth and wisdom are not always aligned. However, beyond having enough food, there is little correlation between monetary wealth and happiness. There *is* a correlation between spiritual abundance and happiness, and this is where Ishtar gets it right.

## Dreams of Money on a New Moon

**KEY THOUGHT:** Follow your heart, find your bliss

With the understanding that dreams of money relate to spiritual riches and that dreams on the new moon present a blank slate of ideas, you have been offered a unique opportunity for creativity, whatever the stress or negativity in your dream.

Many have argued that the best thing money can buy is freedom, yet it has been said that freedom is having nothing left to lose. These two statements appear to be opposites, but Ishtar disagrees. She believes that freedom is a state of mind. Through dreams of money on the new moon, she is saying that no matter the resources, you can export avenues of wealth simply by asking, "What is my pleasure?"

Another well-known saying about work goes, "Follow your heart, find your bliss." This is more Ishtar's style.

## Dreams of Money on a Waxing Crescent Moon

**KEY THOUGHT:** Invest in your spiritual wellbeing

As the sun' light begins to creep around the evening moon, opportunities begin to emerge and become a reality. This is the general impression that the waxing crescent moon emits; opportunities to be pursued.

The dream of money on the waxing crescent moon is a clear message: you have the drive to make things happen, and while not everything may yet be in your control, the desire is unmistakable.

Examine the dream's details carefully if you need more specifics. Are you in debt? Are you owed money? Are you happy with the dreamed finances or stressed about them? Regardless, Ishtar is to be trusted. She isn't telling you just to cause panic – remember that even a worry-filled dream about debt with a palpable similarity to real-life situations should be seen as a gift.

Debt may relate to things that are due. Tasks? Communications? Home projects? Personal connections? There are always things you can do to improve your situation.

Whatever the narrative and emotion you felt in your dream, now is a time to invest in your spiritual wellbeing.

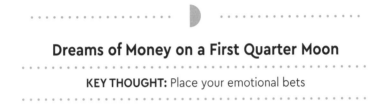

## Dreams of Money on a First Quarter Moon

**KEY THOUGHT:** Place your emotional bets

Money can be your best friend or your biggest source of worry. It can be the motivator for collabouration and the cause of disputes. It is both everything and nothing, leading to a complex relationship.

Dreams of money on the first quarter moon – a phase of split personality – challenge you to be clear in all your dealings. Dreams about money are (most likely) not about money but, instead, options, freedom and security. So, when you consider what "dealings" Ishtar is bringing to your attention via your dreams, search your emotional and spiritual landscape for clues.

In matters of the heart, soul and spirit, reflect on the financial state of affairs in your dream, superimpose that state on your waking challenges and see where you should budget your time, energy and creativity.

Now isn't the time for indecision: you must place your emotional bets.

# Dreams of Money on a Waxing Gibbous Moon

**KEY THOUGHT:** Balance your spiritual budget

Often during work projects, home improvements or creative pursuits, you need to budget before you start the work. You have to consider more than the finances, as time and convenience also play a significant role. While you budget with the best of intentions, it is rare for a first draft to remain intact and unchanged.

Dreams of money on the waxing gibbous moon tell you that tweaks are usually required, except that Ishtar's concern isn't financial but emotional. When you look at your portfolio of security, confidence, time, peace of mind, family, friends and lovers, all must be balanced.

If you need to sacrifice a little social time and put in a few extra hours of overtime to take that yoga retreat, that's a simple tweak you can make to ease your stress. At times it may be more challenging to identify what you need and easier to spot what you don't need. Either one gets you closer to your goal.

You will be more secure if you balance your spiritual budget.

# Dreams of Money on a Full Moon

**KEY THOUGHT:** Cash in or settle up

How many times have you seen a magic trick and wanted to know how it was done, and if shown, how many times did you wish you hadn't been shown? Seeing the full picture can sometimes be an anticlimax. Yet, with dreams on the full moon – when its energy, beauty and power peak are about to start waning – you are encouraged to interpret this peak as a time of acceptance.

When you dream of money, you dream of spiritual wealth. It is important that you review the details of the dream, explore the emotional experiences and see what role loans, debts, abundance and scarcity play in your psyche. Do you owe someone an apology? Do your co-workers undervalue you? Do you owe a debt of gratitude to someone? Do you have a rich social life at the expense of poor time management?

This dream provides an excellent spiritual snapshot or "statement" of who you are, and just like the magic trick, you may wish you hadn't seen it. But the truth is, you can't drive blind, and seeing your statement gives you the opportunity to accept the balance and make informed decisions on the journey toward your best life.

If you are ahead, you can cash in. If you are behind, you should settle up.

## Dreams of Money on a Waning Gibbous Moon

**KEY THOUGHT:** Are you in exchange?

As the shadow of the mood begins to creep across its surface, dark times loom. It can feel dispiriting when things are on the decline, but just as autumn is a critical part of nature's cycle of life, the ebbing and flowing of your rhythms keep you balanced.

Dreams of money on the waning gibbous moon give you the opportunity to reconcile your pursuits to ensure that you are on track, prioritize correctly and feel secure that you are in control of the game of life.

One particular area of life that you can reconcile is your personal and professional relationships. Being "in exchange" is essential when dealing with others. If a relationship feels strained, it may be because one side may feel they are investing more than the other. The simple question, "Do you feel we are in exchange?", can prompt incredibly healthy conversations about the give and take – the interpersonal transactions – of a relationship and make them more balanced and rewarding.

# Dreams of Money on a Third Quarter Moon

**KEY THOUGHT:** Spend less time on unfulfilling activities

No one is so wealthy that they can afford everything. The idea of budgeting is familiar to everyone, and this applies not just to money. Time management, emotional investment and even how much sleep we can afford are all examples of how we budget.

Dreams of money on the third quarter moon challenge you to look at your emotional pie chart to see where you should budget.

An old business coach used to tell me, "There are three ways to increase profits; earn more, spend less, or both." Dreams of money are, of course, not about money; they are about emotional resources, the expenditure of energy and the profit and loss of interpersonal relationships. But the coach's wisdom still applies.

While the overall trajectory that you want to be on is personal growth, this specific dream is Ishtar's way of saying that while you are earning well, you could do with spending less.

Investing in unrewarding or toxic relationships is an energy drain. Distancing yourself from these situations is an example of spending less. Spending less time on social media so you can spend more time in the garden is another.

Spending less time on unfulfilling activities is a great way to increase life's profit margin.

# Dreams of Money on a Waning Crescent Moon

**KEY THOUGHT:** Submit your spiritual tax return

Dreams of money on the waning crescent moon are Ishtar's way of submitting your emotional tax return.

In life, you win some and you lose some, and over time you may get so caught up in the journey that you don't get a chance to breathe. One toxic component of this treadmill lifestyle is debt. Being in debt can gnaw at you; likewise, being owed money or favours can be almost equally debilitating.

Any accountant will tell you that there comes a time in any ledger when debts become more debilitating than their settlement is worth. Writing off bad debts is the simple action taken. And while the accountant may not "forget", they *can* forgive.

When you dream of money in the waning crescent moon, you are projecting a financial face onto your emotional dealings. Whatever drama unfolds within the dream can inform you of profound truths about your life and your attitude toward them.

You should try to avoid starting the new emotional year spiritually overdrawn. By forgiving bad debts – letting go of draining friendships – you save your energy for better things. By paying what you owe – saying "thank you", "I love you" or "I appreciate your work" – you keep your social credit rating in good standing. By paying your spiritual tax obligation – by simply being kind whenever possible – you can define the emotional infrastructure of your world on your terms.

# Nakedness

Humans have a pretty comical relationship with nakedness. Since being born naked is something every human that ever lived has in common, you would think we would be a little more comfortable with it.

Children usually care very little about what they are – or aren't – wearing, but for adults, nudity and intimacy are closely linked. For many tribes throughout history who sought oneness with nature, including many Native Americans, clothes were a spiritual barrier and only nudity allowed them to feel fully in tune with the earth. Nudist communities speak of the joy and freedom of living "*au naturel*".

You may feel more connected to others once you shed your metaphorical garments. Increased familiarity with who someone is, which only happens after we "let down our guard", typically causes more empathy and compassion. Understanding the "real" person comes with profound benefits, even if you learn about behavioural traits you don't like.

Imagine everyone you meet as an oyster, clammed up at first yet carrying within them pearls of wisdom born from the grit and sand of experience. It is only once people open up that their natural beauty and originality can be celebrated; everything else is masquerade.

But this is not the culture in which we live. We have become a t-shirt-and-jeans, or a black-dress-and-heels, kind of species that shuns our true, honest form.

They don't call it "the naked truth" for nothing.

· · · · · · · · · · · · · ◯ · · · · · · · · · · · · ·

## Dreams of Nakedness on a New Moon

**KEY THOUGHT:** Know your strengths and play to them

The new moon is a blank slate filled with potential. Nothing has been defined yet; its details and character are hidden, cloaked in darkness, under wraps. This idea of cloaks hiding our true identity sits at the core of a dream of nakedness. The "co-incidence" of this dream occurring on the new moon is, of course, no coincidence. Ishtar has a reason for everything.

Dreams of nakedness on the new moon are messages that you should become more in touch with your true self. In nearly all instances, open honesty and learning the naked truth about someone is preferable to learning later that their smile is fake. When you are honest with your feelings, opinions and personality, you don't need to worry about the risk of being exposed.

Knowing your strengths and playing to them is the key to confidence.

## Dreams of Nakedness on a Waxing Crescent Moon

**KEY THOUGHT:** Remove masks of pretence

Generally, dreams of nakedness offer a stark reminder that we spend most of our public life with most of our body concealed. And when I say body, I mean every facet of our physical, emotional, psychological and spiritual being. Ishtar sends these dreams as a reminder that you don't need to let that define you and that society, not the universe, sold you the idea of covering up.

The timing of the dream is interesting in that the waxing crescent moon, previously cloaked in darkness, is now shining with silver light, slowly revealing its surface details. Take inspiration from the message of the dream that opening up in your relationships is a healthy journey that doesn't need to be rushed. Removing masks of pretence little by little is a practice that will win you greater acceptance over time.

## Dreams of Nakedness on a First Quarter Moon

**KEY THOUGHT:** Allow yourself to be more authentic

One of the most well-known stories of split personalities is that of *Dr Jekyll and Mr Hyde*. Good and evil struggling for dominance is a familiar trope that can be seen on global levels down to personal struggles.

Dreams of nakedness (being exposed) on the first quarter moon (when its visible surface is half in light and half in shadow) present a clear message illuminating a struggle with authenticity.

Just as charity begins at home, so does authenticity. We rob our culture of so much open beauty by hiding who we are. It is one thing to put on a show at work, and in many ways we are *expected* to "be professional" – not our default state. It is also natural to put our best foot forward in social situations.

Ask yourself: "Am I leading an authentic life?" Denial is a terrible burden. Authenticity is the answer, and home is the place to start. You can and should allow yourself to be more authentic, and if there is one place you should and must be 100 per cent authentic, it is in your own mind.

## Dreams of Nakedness on a Waxing Gibbous Moon

**KEY THOUGHT:** Dress for success

Being exposed as a fraud makes many people anxious at some point in their lives. From social circles in school to capabilities at work, the pressure to thrive (or appear to thrive) is always present, and arguably now more than ever. With its relentless stream of perfect selfies, gorgeous holiday destinations and mouthwatering restaurant dishes, social media reminds us of the standards against which our lives are judged.

The term FOMO – Fear Of Missing Out – describes one form of performance anxiety, but there are many others. Add to the list the insidious influence of Photoshop, which fine-tunes bodies to aspirational (read: unattainable) degrees, and we have to ask ourselves why we do this. The term "fake it till you make it" is an obnoxious corporate slogan to bolster workers fatigued by our modern social pressures.

But it's not all bad news. There are many ways to tweak your presentation and move out of the feeling of "imposter syndrome", because this is what dreams of nakedness on the waxing gibbous moon are all about. Ishtar is telling you that who you are naturally is perfectly good enough and that minor upgrades can work wonders.

Think of it as "dress for success", encouraging you to be a more polished version of yourself. If you can do this, you don't need to fake it, and as far as Ishtar is concerned, if you can do this, you have already made it.

## Dreams of Nakedness on a Full Moon

**KEY THOUGHT:** Let your true characteristics shine

Nakedness on the full moon. If you don't know what "mooning" is, look it up. Jokes aside, there is a powerful message in dreams of nakedness on the full moon – you must let your true characteristics shine. There is no need to hide behind clothes and clouds; the full, honest picture is the most beautiful.

It is as simple as that.

## Dreams of Nakedness on a Waning Gibbous Moon

**KEY THOUGHT:** Where are you exposed to harm?

With this dream category more than any other, there is a stark difference between the interpretation of dreams of nakedness during the waxing and waning phases of the lunar cycle. In the waxing phase, these dreams encourage confidence in revealing your true self, but dreams during the waning gibbous moon speak more "*in* confidence" and cautiously about what you should and shouldn't reveal.

Dreams of nakedness on the waning gibbous contain messages of caution. Not everything you see of the moon is enlightened; you must be aware of a shadow of doubt. Your nakedness in your dream could suggest that you will be exposed to these doubts, lies or other negative judgements in your waking life and are vulnerable.

Think about where in your life you may feel overly keen to be open, as now is a good time to apply the brakes and focus on that relationship. Think about if any areas of your heart may be overexposed and vulnerable, at best to the thoughtlessness of others or at worst to their abuse.

## Dreams of Nakedness on a Third Quarter Moon

**KEY THOUGHT:** Beware of wolves in sheep's clothing

If you have been to a masquerade party, you will relate to the joys of anonymity, and if you have been bullied by online "trolls", you will be painfully aware of the dark side of operating undercover.

Dreams of nakedness on the third quarter moon present a challenging dilemma and a potentially toxic game. To act in secret can be thrilling, but being caught "with your trousers down", so to speak, is a shameful experience and possibly hurtful to others.

In life, we are met with many temptations that may be harmless or harmful to ourselves or others. We may try to live a perfect life, or maybe we don't try. Perhaps we try to live an exciting life, as most of us take risks. While we may risk exposing ourselves and causing harm when we act this way, there is usually a greater danger of others exposing themselves and causing harm to us, simply due to the number of people with whom we interact.

A straightforward way to summarize Ishtar's message would be, "Beware of wolves in sheep's clothing".

## Dreams of Nakedness on a Waning Crescent Moon

**KEY THOUGHT:** Button up

As the lunar cycle enters its final phase, dreams of nakedness represent an opportunity to deal with messy situations, seek closure and tidy up.

The nakedness in the dream speaks to your exposure to the elements, the judgement of others and your unreadiness to face your peers in a conventional way. While some people may enjoy the disruptive effect of these actions, it is more common not to want to negotiate undressed as it would draw attention to the wrong things.

"Button up" has two meanings: the first is to "repress or inhibit something", and the second is to "complete or conclude something satisfactorily".

Sometimes you must do the former to achieve the latter.

# Poop

The way we digest our food is analogous to the way we digest life. We ingest it, we assimilate the healthy elements, we eliminate the waste, and we dispose of it. At least, this is the desired way to do things.

While few of us would consider retrieving our physical waste once we have disposed of it, it is remarkable how many of us retrieve and wallow in our emotional, psychological or psychic waste. Framed in this way, it is easy to see that emotional wallowing isn't a healthy practice. Yet it often takes prompting to realize this is what we are doing. Letting go of negative emotions is easier said than done, starting with awareness.

This is what Ishtar is doing with your dreams about poop; making you aware. As with all dream categories, there are general meanings and numerous specifics that we don't have the space to address in detail in this book. But with practice and familiarity with the general ideas, we can all become more skilled at identifying the specific messages from our particular dream. Here is a quick top-level summary:

Poop is a private matter, and dreams of pooping in public may relate to a violation of privacy in your waking life. Using a dirty toilet in your dreams reflects your negative feelings toward others or situations from which you may wish to distance yourself. Flushing or disposing of waste represents burying negative emotions. A child's poop represents a reluctance to accept responsibility, and playing with it in a dream can suggest anxiety and not letting go of your problems.

Just as how we poop relates to how we live life as individuals, how a culture deals with it provides insight on a cultural level. The Babylonians left it in the streets, the Mesopotamians introduced clay sewerage pipes, and the Romans engineered the first sewerage systems. The Englishman Sir Thomas Crapper pioneered the first flushing toilet. (Yes, that's where the name came from.) We are far more private and clean these days, aiding in our desire to hide our waste.

There is also a strong correlation between dreams of poop and money. Finances are a private matter. Some people regard money as dirty, some think it distasteful to discuss, while others consider lack of it as shameful. It is everyone's little secret.

Shame is a toxic emotion. You would be better off purging yourself of such feelings. Dreams of poop are Ishtar's way of keeping you regular.

## Dreams of Poop on a New Moon

**KEY THOUGHT:** Fight clean from this point forward

Dreams of poop on the new moon are a caution that you should start new endeavours with honesty. The new moon sets things in motion; this is when you begin to develop your ideas. Creation takes time and requires removing blocks. Ishtar is reminding you that your dreams are beautiful, and it is time to wipe the slate clean and create. Whatever your track record may be is in the past. Moving forward, you should maintain an "honesty is the best policy" attitude.

Whether it is complete openness in communications, finances or taking responsibility for one's own decisions, no more little secrets, denials or evasion of ownership of mistakes.

This dream isn't about past transgressions. Ishtar wants you to be happy and believes that fighting clean from this point forward is an opportunity to advance toward your best life.

## Dreams of Poop on a Waxing Crescent Moon

**KEY THOUGHT:** Treachery abounds

As the moon transitions from full shadow, and light begins to illuminate what was once secret, you can start to see a picture emerge. This picture may or may not be all you want it to be. Dreams of poop on the waxing crescent suggest that secrets – possibly hidden secrets – are afoot, a picture that may soon emerge.

Look for clues in the dream. Whose mess did you dream about? If you walked into a dirty bathroom in the dream, you should consider the people around you or the company you work for to see if you are liable for other people's mistakes. If it is your mess in the dream and you are in a public place, you should examine your behaviour. What might you be ashamed of if the truth comes out? And who might see that as an opportunity to shame you?

Either way, treachery could be in play.

## Dreams of Poop on a First Quarter Moon

**KEY THOUGHT:** Open up

The first quarter moon is a dichotomy. Is it illuminated or in shadow, black or white, coming or going? It is all these things, but it won't be for long. It will soon be illuminated. It is currently in doubt and is on its way to committal, and this is the message you are receiving: to commit. But to what?

A dream of poop is an awkward but common one, pointing you to examine more private things in your waking life. Whether this is finances, relationships or even your sexuality and gender identity, things kept secret – kept in the shadows – tend to erode your soul.

The truth is, the truth will out regardless of your efforts to conceal it. The irony is that opening up about money problems, relationship issues, health challenges or your sexuality tend to bring incredible relief and garner support. So, commit to illuminate.

Ishtar wants you to be happy and live in the light. She wants you to open up like a flower. You will be glad you did.

## Dreams of Poop on a Waxing Gibbous Moon

### KEY THOUGHT: Clear the air

Dreams of poop represent the hidden, uncomfortable or secretive parts of your life, or the lives of others, that are troubling your subconscious. Dreams on the waxing gibbous suggest an almost complete picture where few but still some questions remain. This dream at this moment points to the shadow that remains on the gibbous moon and hints that not all is as it should be.

This dream is Ishtar's way of cautioning you that relationships you are in – personal, business or otherwise – are not all they appear to be. If the lurking problem isn't addressed, things could get messy.

You need to review the details of the dream to seek clues about the problem's whereabouts. Replay the dream and consider the circumstances of the experience. An unclean public bathroom suggests irresponsibility in others, to see your own waste represents your own secrets, and flushing it away suggests you are burying your emotions or aren't open to other people's ideas.

The good news is that the picture is almost complete: these issues aren't deal-breakers. The situation just requires a little push of honest communication to clear the air.

## Dreams of Poop on a Full Moon

### KEY THOUGHT: Life is messy. Accept it rather than wallow

The full moon represents a time to accept that the picture is complete, whole and as bright as it will get. While things in your life may not have always turned out perfectly, your attitude toward 90 per cent success or even 50 per cent can radically change your outlook on life and your enjoyment. In fact, a good attitude toward a zero per cent success can be viewed as a 100 per cent learning experience. The full moon is the time to invest energy in your attitude toward the picture you see.

But what if the picture is unsavoury?

Dreams of poop are about mess – yours or someone else's – that is unpleasant. So, dreams of poop on the full moon suggest that the picture you see is a troubling one that requires cleaning up.

You can complain or roll up your sleeves and work to improve the situation. No one wants mess, but it is a fact of life. The variable is what you choose to do about it.

Dreams of poop on the full moon are Ishtar's way of reminding you that life is messy and to accept it rather than wallow.

## Dreams of Poop on a Waning Gibbous Moon

**KEY THOUGHT:** Pull up weeds when you see them

The waning gibbous moon is the lunar phase when shadow starts to creep over what was once a perfect picture. Dreams of poop suggest that things may not be as clean as you want them to be. Shadows, lies, secrets, withholds, financial deceit, infidelity or any other messy behaviours may be encroaching on what was a good thing. You should look around you and within yourself to see if you can identify the source.

If you look closely at the circumstances of the dream – whose mess you were dealing with, what was done about it, how you felt, etc. – these can help you identify what Ishtar is hinting at.

The moon is still bright and the shadows are growing. These may not represent deep, dark toxicity. These things often start as innocent assumptions, misunderstandings, fatigue or laziness. But if these aren't nipped in the bud, and instead are allowed to fester, this is when things get messy.

If you keep your side of the street clean and pull up weeds when you see them, you can maintain a healthy garden.

## Dreams of Poop on a Third Quarter Moon

**KEY THOUGHT:** Flush negativity

There is a great deal of uncertainty with the third quarter moon, an uncertainty that doesn't serve well. Shadows are growing, and this lunar phase prompts you to make clear-cut decisions as they approach.

Why? Because if you don't, things could get messy.

The truth is, dreams about poop are gifts. They are messages from Ishtar that your body is telling you to be guided to protect against negative situations that may affect your wellbeing. It is time to speak out – and decisively – to rid yourself of whatever is unsavoury and seek a clean slate, a fresh start.

You innately know what you need to do. You should consider what needs to be removed from your life, learn to express your emotions and listen to Ishtar and your intuition.

The more cleanly you can live your emotional lives, the fewer weeds will grow. The more you can rid yourself of the negative, the better.

In a word: flush.

## Dreams of Poop on a Waning Crescent Moon

**KEY THOUGHT:** Tidy up with integrity

As the lunar cycle draws to an end, the waning crescent shows you its remaining light in the pre-dawn hours. It is getting late, so if you are to make any changes to your planes, now is the time for final touches.

With dreams of poop comes a message from Ishtar that things aren't as clean as they could be. Honest, transparent, responsible conduct is something you should expect not just from others but from yourself toward others.

As the moon fades, you have a chance to close the chapter the right way. If you owe apologies to others, offer them. If other people owe you an apology, you may or may not get one – you can't control the actions of others – but you can state calmly how the behaviour has hurt you so they are aware of their actions' impact .

By tidying up, you define your quality and integrity to the universe and manifest that you are treated the same.

# Pregnancy and Birth

Pregnancy dreams are often about shedding light on the shadows within yourself so that you can understand what needs to be realized and needs to be born. The challenge is to find the courage to face your fears and trust your intuition, to step out into the light and embark on a new journey.

Mothers-to-be often find themselves dreaming of being pregnant. It is extremely common and very understandable. Childbirth represents a major shift – for the parents as well as the baby – and dreams of pregnancy foresee the same; major shifts requiring major reflection. What are you offering the world? What are you creating? How are you developing and growing internally? The dream calls on you to reflect on all of these questions.

It is not just pregnant women who have these thoughts. At heart, this dream is a message that something will be born: a new approach or project. Many people have or will at some point embark upon labours of love so intense that their conception through completion feels akin to pregnancy. They may use the same words for these endeavours, such as conception, gestation, delivery, etc. And how often do people refer to their book, invention, home or artwork as their "baby"? It's not surprising that these labours of love can evoke dreams of pregnancy.

From the Nativity to the Renaissance – each derived from *natal*, meaning birth – the birth of humans, civilizations, ideas, projects and enlightenment are all up for consideration when we interpret dreams of pregnancy and childbirth.

Ishtar knows that the desire to create from nothing but desire and collabouration is a powerful instinct. The fear of failure, too, becomes heightened; there is no way around it. The stakes are high, and your anxiety will always match the stakes.

It would be hard to imagine how this intensity would *not* stir your subconscious, spiritual and emotional self. It is equally difficult to imagine that Ishtar wouldn't have something to say about that.

## Dreams of Pregnancy and Birth on a New Moon

**KEY THOUGHT:** Imagine without limits

There is perhaps no page in this book that so strongly points to creativity, new endeavours and life transformation than this one. Dreams of pregnancy and birth on the new moon speak to pure potential, uncertainty in the end result and the anxiety of failure.

Shadows of doubt conceal the moon and your subconscious, hiding any notions of the expression of your desires. Now is the time to conceive these things, put doubts aside and simply aspire.

Just as you may say to children that they can be anything they want to be and encourage them to work undaunted toward their goals, Ishtar is telling you the same.

Your life experience is limited only by your imagination. Life will put barriers in your way, but don't allow it to do so – imagine without limits.

## Dreams of Pregnancy and Birth on a Waxing Crescent Moon

**KEY THOUGHT:** Take small steps toward your goals

As the shadow of the new moon begins to recede, revealing the waxing crescent moon, you enter a time of the germination of ideas. Dreams of pregnancy and birth reinforce this idea of development and growth, and while there is still far to go, you are on your way.

Whether you are *actually* pregnant, considering a business idea, looking for a more creative outlet or feel unstimulated at work and wishing for more, you may be facing some life challenges that terrify you. Life is complex enough, and the added responsibility of a baby, startup or change of professional direction can present as much anxiety as excitement and can be as daunting as the shadows that darken the surface of the moon.

Ishtar knows that if you are to complete a desired journey, desire alone isn't enough. The next step in your journey is the plan. Just as a journey of 1,000 miles begins with one step, breaking down a big, overwhelming task into many small, doable single-step tasks is the way to go.

Now is the time to take your first step toward your goals. Ishtar doesn't care how quickly you advance, develop and grow; she only cares that you are heading in the right direction. And the easiest and surest way to do that is by taking small steps.

## Dreams of Pregnancy and Birth on a First Quarter Moon

**KEY THOUGHT:** Choose to unlock mind-forged manacles

With dreams of pregnancy and birth on the first quarter moon, you are at a transitional moment in your life when you must choose your destiny. Half shrouded in shadow and half revealed in light, you have unfinished business to attend to – anything that may not be going according to plan.

While new challenges (whether these are an actual pregnancy or a project in development) can bring excitement and responsibility, the fear of failure can be paralyzing. Yet that paralysis is a mind-forged manacle, and the key to this is choice.

In any endeavour, there comes a point when turning back is more harmful than proceeding. With that moment looming, all is still within your control, and you need to make decisions.

## Dreams of Pregnancy and Birth on a Waxing Gibbous Moon

**KEY THOUGHT:** Labour can be hard so remember to breathe

With any labour of love, the preparation may require more "heavy lifting", yet the final touches may be more time-consuming and stressful. You may sometimes be so entrenched in the *doing* that you don't see that only *finishing* is now required.

Dreams of pregnancy and birth on the waxing gibbous moon are signals from Ishtar to transition from the heavy lifting of creation to the detailing.

In practical terms, you can never be 100 per cent ready for your next adventure; in emotional terms, you can. Meditating on your readiness, reassuring yourself that life will never put you into a situation you are ill-equipped to handle, is key to mental preparation.

Labour can be difficult. Remember to breathe.

## Dreams of Pregnancy and Birth on a Full Moon

**KEY THOUGHT:** Peace of mind is the most important ingredient in the formula for success

There are few things more profound than childbirth, yet many people have experienced a sense of anticlimax and even depression after the event. From a broader perspective, the same applies to long-awaited holidays, art projects, professional pursuits or sports.

Babies sleep a lot in the first few weeks. The stillness that follows the high emotional drama of pregnancy isn't what many parents expect, just as people who parachute for the first time find that for all the anxiety of the buildup, the stillness of floating was all the more brilliant.

Dreams of pregnancy and birth on the full moon are signs from Ishtar that no matter what responsibility you are taking on or labour you are engaged in, maintaining peace of mind and a sense of spiritual balance is the formula for success and wellbeing.

## Dreams of Pregnancy and Birth on a Waning Gibbous Moon

**KEY THOUGHT:** Confidence is as easy as Plan-ABC

One of the most exciting things about new ideas is imagining the ideal outcome of your vision. Dreams of pregnancy and birth are rich with symbolic and literal meaning as you develop and grow personally, spiritually, professionally and intellectually. However, as the military saying goes, a plan rarely survives the first shot. This is where contingencies come in so handy.

As you prepare for a baby, an app launch, an art project or a fitness regime, setting goals is of primary importance. Yet this shouldn't downplay the critical role of contingency.

You have made plan A. By asking yourself, "what if . . .?" and making a list of plans B and C, one of two things will happen. If you end up needing plans B and C, you can remain confident that you planned correctly. If you don't end up needing them, you can remain confident that you planned correctly.

And "what if" you don't plan contingencies? All Ishtar wants is for you to be confident. So, why not? Confidence is as easy as Plan-ABC.

## Dreams of Pregnancy and Birth on a Third Quarter Moon

**KEY THOUGHT:** Keep your life goals out of harm's way

Half of all plans to *do* something involve plans to *not* do other things. Anyone with an understanding of "family planning" will get that planning against a circumstance that conflicts with a preferred outcome or schedule is critical to the management of life's journey.

Dreams of pregnancy and birth on the third quarter moon are Ishtar's way of pointing to possible scenarios that happen if you are casual or cavalier in your approach. Planning against undesirable outcomes is like weeding the garden to allow the roses to bloom.

Keeping your children and life goals out of harm's way is your job. Nature will take care of the rest.

## Dreams of Pregnancy and Birth on a Waning Crescent Moon

**KEY THOUGHT:** Nurture your creations with love and patience

In literal terms, pregnancy concludes with the birth of a baby. Metaphorically, the delivery may also be an idea or a business venture. Yet, most people know that any idea or business venture, and of course a baby, requires nurturing.

Bringing an idea to fruition is step one. Raising it to reach its full potential is the journey on which you now embark.

Dreams of pregnancy and birth on the waning crescent moon are a message from Ishtar that you acknowledge and accept the responsibility of caring for yourself, and your ideas, creations, personal relationships, family and garden if you wish these to flourish.

The grass isn't always greener on the other side; it is greener where it is watered. You must feed your creations with love and patience.

# Sex

There is perhaps no more repressive global taboo than conversation about sex. This isn't just a contemporary trait. Dating back before the Mesopotamian era, humans have frowned upon healthy discussion on the topic, but just because we can't talk freely about our desires doesn't mean we don't have them. This social repression makes the subject open season for our subconscious and vibrant source material for our dreams.

Sexual dreams shock the system like no other, thanks to their taboo-busting nature. We can sometimes be vainly flattered or superficially aroused by their literal suggestion or mistakenly project more importance than we should on the physical nature of the idea. However, Ishtar could care less about the physicality of sex – or the physicality of *anything*, for that matter. Physicality is not her realm. Her focus is on our emotional and psychological wellbeing – regardless of the subject of our dream – and it is often more insightful if we can keep this in mind as we dig for meaning.

Ishtar herself was not only the Mesopotamian goddess of dreams but also of sexual pleasure, love, beauty, justice, war and power. These are all linked on a psychological level. As such, sexual dreams are most likely messages that we are seeking answers or external desires in the waking world and that we should focus on what we want out of life.

A general cheat sheet for those in a relationship reads as follows: ejaculation equates to "purpose" and where to direct our energy; phalluses represent the cultivation of power (in whatever form our subconscious feels we could benefit); and infidelity equates to insecurity. While dreams of infidelity are almost certainly *not* a predictor of *actual* infidelity, they *are* a nudge toward better communication.

For our single brothers and sisters, a general guide is that sexual dreams pertain to unmet desires on a broader front, whether these are career, love, touch or any other pursuit.

Dreams of sex with someone who isn't committed can be interpreted as encouragement to be more forthcoming and open about your fears. Dreams of someone you don't desire, once you get over the shock of the idea, can point you toward exploring areas of difficulty you may be experiencing with your current lover.

With all that said, much more remains to be divined when you note the timing of your dream in the lunar cycle.

## Dreams of Sex on a New Moon

**KEY THOUGHT:** Consider your choices in life

Dreaming of sex on the new moon is a clear signal that it may be time for you to turn a new page in the book of love.

Remember; in life you always have a choice. You choose – consciously or unconsciously – to perpetuate bad habits, put up a shield indefinitely to "protect" yourself from pain, or work toward a goal of enjoying healthy relationships. In this dream, Ishtar asks you to be conscious of your choices. And her timing is impeccable.

She may be saying: Is it time to experiment? Is it time to seek deeper connections with those you already know? What is standing in the way of your satisfaction? Given the fundamental importance of such questions, it may be worth investing a moment of your day to consider your choices.

## Dreams of Sex on a Waxing Crescent Moon

**KEY THOUGHT:** Pursue your best self

Sexual dreams on a waxing crescent moon are signs that Ishtar is nudging you to pursue your desires. There is much excitement and opportunity during this lunar phase. Add to that the innate excitement revealed in dreams of a sexual nature and the "coincidence" of the dream, and the timing is very dynamic.

It is certainly not merely a coincidence. Oh no; Ishtar is wiser than that. Sex dreams on a waxing crescent moon tell you she wants you to make your move! Now is the time to plan what you really want so that you can grow and attract what you desire. Now is the time to put plans in place.

Swipe right, ask directly, speak up, be proactive, invite the possibility of more, open the door to opportunity. There are many ways the waxing crescent moon can influence you. The way you manifest Ishtar's inspiration to improve your life and create more varied, rewarding partnerships is up to you. How wonderful is that? But it is worth nothing unless you act upon your motivations. It is up to you to manifest it.

It should also be noted that a dream of *great* sex during the waxing crescent moon – no matter who your dream partner happened to be – is a good sign that you have opportunities to take more ownership and control of your vulnerabilities. Ishtar says that you can be *more*. She knows you *want* to be more. And she is telling you that you should pursue your best self. It is a nice dream, for sure. And what is even *nicer* is that you get to *then* ask yourself if you are giving your existing relationship the attention it deserves.

Only Ishtar and the waxing crescent moon together could be so kind as to bring such a gentle message of self-awareness delivered in such a fun way.

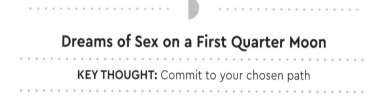

## Dreams of Sex on a First Quarter Moon

**KEY THOUGHT:** Commit to your chosen path

A time of assessment is practically the definition of the first quarter moon. The moon seeks commitment, and so do your dreams during this lunar phase. With dreams of a sexual nature at this time in the lunar cycle, you are being guided to assess the areas of intimacy in your life and question your commitment to them.

Ishtar has no opinion on the matter – she works for you – but she may know you better than you know yourself and can usually see opportunities you can't. Negative emotions, resistance, past wounds, blind optimism, lust and infatuation are all enemies of reality and your deeper wellbeing. When you have sexual dreams on the first quarter moon, she prompts you to check in with yourself. After that, the decision is yours.

A sexual dream during this quarter should inspire you to walk a path to love that is clear and brightly lit, not obscured by shadows of doubt.

## Dreams of Sex on a Waxing Gibbous Moon

**KEY THOUGHT:** Enlighten up and work toward your bliss

With such a complex subject matter as intimacy, you can often take things that pertain to your psychological wellbeing so seriously that you forget that your purpose in life is to experience joy and not take yourself too seriously. Taking joy seriously is both critically important and a nonsensical contradiction. But you know what I mean. Dreams of sex on a waxing gibbous moon remind you that you are so close to pure joy that you should now only focus on fine-tuning what you have and work toward bliss.

Dreams on the waxing gibbous moon remind you to be at ease while working out what you want in your relationships. Trust in the power and inspiration of the dream to keep you on track, have fun in life and reflect on what tweaks you could make.

Counterintuitively, it is a great time to be alone and meditate on your desires.

## Dreams of Sex on a Full Moon

**KEY THOUGHT:** Manage your relationship expectations

For most of this book, I have steered clear of discussing how the menstrual cycle relates to the lunar phases. But it would be remiss of me not to bring it up here.

Since pre-recorded history, and first documented in Babylon through Ishtar's interest in fertility and rebirth, humans have associated the full moon with the womb. Even the word menstrual is derived from the Greek word *mene*, meaning moon. Many cycles synchronize with the moon; hormone levels – ovulation and sexual desires – are heightened and emotions can be elevated during a dynamic time.

Dreams of sex on the full moon are not uncommon, but that doesn't dilute their potency. Now is a time to take stock of current relationships, accept them for what they are and check in with your expectations. There are no unsuccessful relationships, only unmet expectations. If you can manage your expectations, you can rule your world.

## Dreams of Sex on a Waning Gibbous Moon

**KEY THOUGHT:** Seek ways to recharge existing bonds

Though the waning gibbous moon is now receding, it is still bright and almost complete. Likewise, sex dreams during this phase are a positive message that pruning and editing your relationships are healthy practices.

These dreams at these times ask you to seek an understanding, or at least an acknowledgement, of past mistakes. Ishtar wants you to bring about any changes you deem relevant for your future development and health, and this dream at this time is a prompt to do that.

You have the opportunity to forge new paths – new relationships – and with each new day, you can use what you have learned to take the next step with greater confidence. This dream moment reminds you to seek ways to recharge existing bonds with fresh energy. This recharging doesn't need to be intense or emotionally charged. Take it easy. Take the heat out. Think; passion without the strings, adult without the triple-X.

A sexual dream during the waxing gibbous moon is a message to be happy with the present. Don't worry about the future; you have got this.

# Dreams of Sex on a Third Quarter Moon

**KEY THOUGHT:** What is hindering your growth?

The moon is divided; it is decision time. Sexual dreams pertain to your general desires, met or unmet. The third quarter moon is a time of transition: black and white. Are you in or out? It is a potent moment, and Ishtar knows it. She suggests that you are at a crossroads and it is time to sever negative ties.

These negative ties may be a person, an aspect of a relationship or even an element of your unconscious self that compromises your wellbeing or hijacks good intentions (such as trepidation or lust). Ishtar doesn't care what *it* is. She cares that something is in your way and asks that you remove it.

Take a look around you and ask yourself what is standing in your way. If you can find the clarity of mind to identify something – *anything* – that hinders your development, now is the time to muster the strength to do something about it.

This action doesn't need to be dramatic. We can all learn to navigate our relationships with more skill, and often it just requires minor, frequent adjustments. Just as with driving, if we have a general destination in mind, all we then need to do is avoid the ditches. Sexual dreams on the third quarter moon are a call for you to avoid the ditches on your emotional journey.

## ☾

### Dreams of Sex on a Waning Crescent Moon

**KEY THOUGHT:** Seek to heal old emotional wounds

Memories of past relationships can be painful unless and until you resolve them, forgive transgressions, heal properly and move on. Few people are qualified psychologists, but most intuitively understand that if they don't appropriately file their hurts in the "managed" folder, these will keep popping up to mess with them. Sexual dreams on the waning crescent moon are the perfect sign that Ishtar believes you may benefit from a bit of filing of unresolved issues.

Take a moment to think of your personal relationship with intimacy with others – physical or emotional – and seek areas of discomfort. (These often disguise themselves as things you say you "don't care" about, so look carefully and be honest.) If you find anything you blame someone else for, this is a red flag and you should dig deeper; you may be onto something. Your blame toward someone else may be a false balm for an unresolved emotional wound of your own. In truth, cracks are where the light comes in. Feeling pain is your body's way of saying, "This can heal."

It is said that light is the best antiseptic, and this is good advice. This exercise of identifying discomfort helps us to identify areas where healing may not yet be complete.

Take Ishtar's cues and be well.

# Sharks

Primal, apex predators, ruthless and tireless hunters, the undisputed master of their environment – humans have surpassed all evolutionary expectations.

You may have thought I was going to say sharks. The same adjectives apply, and in some ways, sharks and humans are similar in how both species are dominant in their own worlds. But there lies the distinction. Dry land is the domain of humans, and the ocean is the domain of sharks.

Two-thirds of the planet is covered in water, and sharks have been the kings of their world for 400 million years. They predate the dinosaurs and have changed little since then. When a catastrophic meteor hit the earth 66 million years ago, it rewound the evolution of land-based life from dinosaurs back to shrews. In practical terms, land life had to start all over again. No such rewind occurred for ocean-based life. Sharks were the dinosaurs of the ocean then and still are now, unchanged for about one-tenth of the existence of our planet.

Sharks are the undisputed masters of the seas. They also live rent-free in our limbic system – our primal fight-or-flight brain – as an icon of hostility, greed and unscrupulous consumption, driven purely by gain and utterly vacant of emotion. The sharks' uncanny sense of smell – for blood, no less – and its almost supernatural hunting abilities have inspired folk tales and mysticism alike. The wearing of a shark tooth necklace, for example, was regarded for centuries as a good luck omen for sailors, not just to ward off adversity but also to help them reach their destination still shipshape. In short, sharks live in human subconscious and feed on human fear.

When Ishtar notices these emotions swimming around your subconscious, for whatever reason, she projects them into your dreams. Your conscious mind – a master of pattern recognition – then takes that information and reads "shark".

## Dreams of Sharks on a New Moon

**KEY THOUGHT:** Never stop fighting for what you want in life

When you dream on the new moon, the messages these dreams contain are framed in the context of creativity, the conception of new ideas and being open to all possibilities: a fresh start. It is within this context that dreams of sharks should be considered. Dreams of sharks, shark attacks, bites and menace are neither literal nor prophetic; they are the conscious interpretation of emotions swimming in your subconscious. Fear, predation, ruthlessness, tireless pursuit and unemotional dominance are reverse-engineered to form the image of the shark.

When you consider these emotions and how they relate to your waking life, you may be able to see that, in life, you could take the role of the shark or the victim. When you look at the important components of your life – work, social, emotional, financial, physical, spiritual, etc. – you may be able to recognize the shark. Are you contemplating an aggressive startup? Are you single and dating purely for sex without consideration for the other? Are you drowning in credit card debt due to high interest rates from loan sharks? If you can identify the shark, you are halfway to dealing with it.

Sharks represent a perfect metaphor for life. You may sometimes feel that the constant struggles you experience in your daily life are similar to the restless search for prey that defines a shark's existence. Always on the lookout for threats, in competition and on high alert to respond to opportunities that require rapid responses, sharks aren't so different. The inspiration you can glean is from their tenacity; they never give up. Likewise, you should never stop fighting for what you want in life.

When you dream of sharks, Ishtar is telling you there is a shark in the water. It sounds like it is time to ask yourself, "Am I a predator? Am I prey?" Neither is healthy, and Ishtar is saying you should never underestimate your opponents. You should always be prepared for anything and ready to fight for what you want.

## Dreams of Sharks on a Waxing Crescent Moon

**KEY THOUGHT:** In a world of fish, be a shark

Dreams on the waxing crescent moon are signals from Ishtar that you are embarking on new ventures. Now is an exciting time to review what you have been considering but have yet to act upon.

Often, when you have an idea in your head – whether a health regime or a business enterprise – it can feel that the first step is the hardest. Or, if not the hardest, certainly one that experiences the most inertia. You may become so paralyzed with the idea that what you intend to do must be perfect that you talk yourself out of even starting. You let doubt and darkness conduct your (in)actions.

If this is the case, dreams of sharks have been sent to shake you out of your stupor. However you interpret your dream's specifics, one thing isn't up for debate: the shark is going after its objective and the objective needs to act quickly. The message is clear: one of two things will happen and the most energetic will win.

Inaction on the shark's part will leave it hungry, while inactivity on the prey's part will leave it eaten.

Ishtar is sending you a wakeup call to get started. It is irrelevant that there are plenty of fish in the sea if you don't at least try to catch them. What would a shark do? It would keep moving ahead, keep searching, keep emotions out of the way and keep believing.

In a world of fish, be a shark.

## Dreams of Sharks on a First Quarter Moon

**KEY THOUGHT:** Facing your fears is the only way to make them go away

The first quarter moon is a time of tension and conflict, black and white, with light, truth, fact and materialization on the ascent, and creativity, doubt, secrets and pessimism being pushed back. But the moon hasn't come to fruition yet; it requires more light.

Dreams of sharks reflect your inner fears of predators, even if the predators are internal. Dreams that relate to worries on the first quarter moon are like monsters that hide under the bed. You can pull the blankets up to your eyes or boldly grab a flashlight and look for yourself.

More often than not, your fears hate the light; they hate the truth. They feed on mystery, fear and hearsay. You can spook them by facing them, and the last thing you should do is run from fear.

Dreams of sharks on the first quarter moon are messages from Ishtar that if you turn to face your fears and even dare to hit back, you will overcome them.

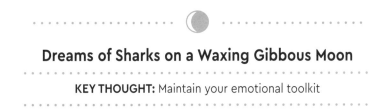

## Dreams of Sharks on a Waxing Gibbous Moon

**KEY THOUGHT:** Maintain your emotional toolkit

Dreams of sharks relate to primal fears, greed and relentless problems circling you. This doesn't necessarily mean you should assume you are the victim. You may be the shark. It is easier (and kinder) to visualize yourself as an innocent victim, but you shouldn't assume you never hurt someone. If you are honest with yourself, you may be more sharklike than you think. The ethics aside, you may also be a shark in business, or in any pursuit for that matter.

Sharks are highly efficient and exceptionally well designed, and they maintain their toolkit. Their teeth, for example, are in a constant state of renewal – emerging, growing, falling out – so their bite is always the sharpest it can be.

We, humans, are like this at a cellular level. Thanks to regeneration, no cell in our body is older than two years. We don't age as a function of time; we are scripted this way. It is a shame we are not like that on an emotional level: refreshed and evolved.

You would do well to reframe negativity in a positive way. Instead of saying you are out of work, you can say you are between jobs. Instead of feeling that problems are constantly circling you, you can regard them as "yet to be dealt with". If you can keep all your emotional spears sharp, you will be in better shape to manage the sharks surrounding you. A steady temper, a healthy attitude, a positive outlook and a spirit of adventure will serve you well and shield you against the septic bite of cynicism.

## Dreams of Sharks on a Full Moon

**KEY THOUGHT:** Most of your concerns are statistically harmless

It is a tragic fact that because of our primal fear of sharks, we treat them harshly. We kill about 100 million sharks annually, yet we still hear news stories of shark attacks. How deadly can they really be? How do we stop them? The truth is that an average of ten reported deaths annually are attributed to shark attacks. Compare that to around 150 deaths a year due to falling coconuts, none of which make the news. The truth is, and the rational conclusion should be, that sharks are statistically harmless.

But tell that to the swimmer who sees a fin in the water.

The implied danger of sharks has far more of an impact on the human psyche than actual danger. There is a wonderful scene in the movie *Jaws* when all the beachgoers panic at the rumour of a shark only to discover that the fin is a child snorkelling.

Only when you take the mask off the monster or look beneath the surface can you properly determine the appropriate response. Dreams of sharks on the full moon are revelations of the big picture, the unmasked emotion of Ishtar's concerns and a moment to review your response.

Are you drowning in debt or just irritated by it? Are you circled by loan sharks and hustlers or just in their part of town? Are you the predator? Do you feel that the fins circling you – the opportunists and the shady dealers – are after you or just after scraps?

When you examine the landscape of your concerns, are you in as much danger as you think? Or are you panicking like the beachgoers in *Jaws*?

Most of the things you worry about are probably statistically harmless.

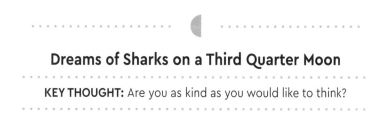

## Dreams of Sharks on a Waning Gibbous Moon

**KEY THOUGHT:** If you smell blood, get out of the water

As shadow begins to creep across the waning crescent moon, we enter the waning phase of the moon. Regard this as the sowing of doubt and trust, the emergence of secrets or the presence of the unscrupulous. It is as if despite the calm, glassy waters of life there is a rumour of a fin.

Dreams of sharks on the waning gibbous moon are cautions from Ishtar that not all is as it seems. In personal or business dealings, can you really be sure of the person with whom you shake hands or kiss for the first time?

So, what can you do?

If you are overcautious, you will never dive into the ocean of desires or opportunity. No matter how many other fish are in the sea, if you fear it you will miss out on much of what life has to offer. Yet if you are too cavalier, you can get hurt.

Your dreams are metaphors, and the reality is that few things you do will put you in mortal danger. Prudence in business and physical safety in matters of the heart are always sage. If you smell blood, if your gut instincts don't feel right, this may be a good time to get out and dry off.

## Dreams of Sharks on a Third Quarter Moon

**KEY THOUGHT:** Are you as kind as you would like to think?

In much of this chapter, I have discussed the psychic overreaction to fear that can cloud your judgement, but there are times when the signs are clear that danger lurks.

Dreams of sharks on the third quarter moon are about as close to prophetic messages as this book is comfortable discussing. Ishtar recognizes the feeling of predatory behaviour circling in your waking life that is reinforced by the timing of the dream. The third quarter moon is a tense transitional moment between light and dark emotions.

This dream could be worrying in several ways, but as with all other dream interpretations in this book, Ishtar is being constructive if you evaluate it carefully enough and divine its message clearly. What is clear is that your subconscious worries have become tangible. It is time to take a moment to review all your personal, business, social and social media relationships and see if you can spot predators.

By the way, you shouldn't assume the shark isn't yourself. The mirror can be a place of jagged truths and shattered self images. Are you as kind as you would like to think?

## Dreams of Sharks on a Waning Crescent Moon

**KEY THOUGHT:** Stop thrashing, and you will know the way

The waning crescent moon is a time on the lunar calendar when you can close chapters, seek resolution and settle debts. Anything that isn't resolved now will come back to bite you. Likewise, dreams of sharks communicate there are fears and predatory behaviours in your circle that are cause for concern.

So, while dreams of sharks on the waning crescent moon are superficially contradictory, the solution is simple: stop thrashing.

Many of the waves we experience in life are of our own making, and much of the unwanted attention we receive is drawn when we project panic, helplessness and noise.

When I was young, I was playing in the ocean and was suddenly hit by a large wave that slammed me onto the ocean floor. I was winded, panicked and tumbled head-over-heels until I lost all sense of direction. Yet as I tumbled, completely confused as to which way was up, I had a moment of clarity; stop panicking and watch the bubbles. And once I saw them, I was able to follow them to the surface.

If you can take a moment each day to stop thrashing, look beyond the chaos and follow the signs you are shown, you will know the way.

# Snakes and Serpents

Snakes are perhaps the most mistrusted animals in the human psyche. To get a handle on what this means, consider being called a snake. What would that imply about your character? Does this mean you are secretive, slippery, covert, disloyal, deceitful, sneaky, slick, hypnotizing, venomous? Snakes possess few positive attributes and the accusation would certainly be unflattering.

Even the shedding of skin, rejuvenation of a kind, could also be a form of disguise or shapeshifting. While any human over a certain age may wish for more youthful skin, the shedding of skin seems a ghastly, alien or dystopian solution. The metaphor of "shedding our skin", meaning changing old ways and revealing a new, real self, can also be unnerving.

Ishtar is more open-minded, though, and dreams of snakes should be seen as much for their positive messages as their negative ones.

The relationship humans have with snakes is long and complex. Most ancient cultures tended to worship or demonize snakes in one way or another, or at least have their deity interact with snakes in religious art.

From Adam and Eve to Medusa, and dating back before recorded history, snakes – or serpents – have had a starring role in the evolution of spiritual thinking. It should be no surprise that they are common and potent players in subconscious and therefore dreams. By displaying such unsettling characteristics (that would be so unwelcome in humans), snakes have become an icon of these traits. What else would you dream of when "man speaks with forked tongue"?

Entrapment, rejuvenation, hidden agendas, charm, changing one's ways, healing, (dis)loyalty and deception are some of the themes you can apply to your interpretation of dreams involving snakes.

## Dreams of Snakes and Serpents on a New Moon

**KEY THOUGHT:** What can you do to live more authentically?

With the new moon comes new possibilities, new ideas and fresh thinking. The idea that you can reinvent yourself is a nice but challenging one that usually requires prompting. You may wait until some milestone event marks a key moment and inspires you. The passing of a loved one, hitting rock bottom or a New Year's resolution are some of the moments of reflection that may make you want to shed your skin and live a more authentic life.

You should add dreams of snakes on the new moon to this list of prompts. The list of negative attributes a snake possesses is long, but the metaphor of it shedding old ways and revealing a new, fresher, rejuvenated self is an exciting one. Through a dream of snakes on the new moon, you can heed Ishtar's message and seek to cast off old habits and replace them with new, freshly considered resolutions.

By "freshly considered", I don't mean engaging in wishful thinking. As snakes shed their old skin, they reveal more authentic versions of themselves. And this is the message the dream of snakes on the new moon contains: to ask what you can do to live more authentically.

# Dreams of Snakes on a Waxing Crescent Moon

**KEY THOUGHT:** Be honest in matters of the heart

As the light of the sun begins to illuminate the edge of the waxing moon, it wraps itself around the shadow of the dark side of the moon in much the same way that a snake wraps its body around its prey. While a snake's actions are predatory, the sun's light can be interpreted as positivity beginning to encircle the shadow of fear and uncertainty.

However, there is a contradiction here. While light illuminates facts and truth, snakes with their forked tongues are often associated with deceit. As the light of the waxing moon increases, Ishtar is telling you that exciting opportunities will come to you that were previously hidden in the long grass, but aspects of these opportunities may still be hidden.

You must ensure that as you pursue your desires you don't turn dark or resort to deception to achieve your goals. This behaviour can be particularly damaging in your love life.

Be cautious of temptation and be honest in matters of the heart.

# Dreams of Snakes and Serpents on a First Quarter Moon

**KEY THOUGHT:** Don't accept no for an answer

Snakes are synonymous with deceit. They can also be slippery and hard to handle. Some challenges in life can be like that: eluding your command of the situation with seemingly endless energy for resisting restraint. Yet snakes are also experts in restraining others, and this duality ties in with the first quarter moon as a time of duelling light and dark traits.

You may often find yourself wrestling with your emotions or with decisions. You can get so caught up in weighing the pros and the cons that you lose perspective; you become paralyzed with indecision.

Dreams of snakes on the first quarter moon represent this struggle between dark and light. If you can muster the energy of the snake to resist constriction due to adversity and instead seek a better grip of whatever the challenge might be, you can regain control.

This is often easier said than done, as it requires energy and the strength to keep fighting.

Don't accept no for an answer.

## Dreams of Snakes and Serpents on a Waxing Gibbous Moon

**KEY THOUGHT:** Prepare for the worst so that you can expect the best

With the waxing gibbous moon, good things are coming. There is only a thin, snake-like crescent of shadow that stands (or lies supine) in the way of the moon's fruition, and the full moon is just days away. But this remaining, subtle shadow of doubt can act like a snake in the grass in that unforeseen obstacles can sometimes block you from your goals.

While having a mortgage fall through or travel plans scuttled at the last minute may be unavoidable, preparing emotionally and logistically for worst-case scenarios isn't, and is more often insurance against them happening. Some people carry an umbrella to ensure good weather. This is a good strategy, especially when rain is frequent but unpredictable. In this dream, this is what Ishtar advises.

Dreams of snakes on the waxing gibbous moon prompt you to prepare for the worst so that you can expect the best.

# Dreams of Snakes and Serpents on a Full Moon

**KEY THOUGHT:** Be still, reflect and have faith

With the moon at its peak, energy is high and gifts and opportunities are plentiful, yet reaching out and seizing opportunities may not always be the best action to take. Sometimes, being still can draw more interest than stomping around making noise. Research shows that snakes are less active during the full moon's bright light, and there are lessons you can take away here.

When you see an opportunity present itself, the message from Ishtar is that you should be still, reflect and have faith that this or a better opportunity is yours.

# Dreams of Snakes and Serpents on a Waning Gibbous Moon

**KEY THOUGHT:** Look out for red flags regarding trust and loyalty

As shadow begins to hide the pristine circle of the full moon, it heralds the waning gibbous phase. Darkness begins to wrap itself around the light, hiding more of what you know and casting doubts on the good.

Just as the sun wakes the cold-blooded snake, the full moon wakes the shadow of the waning gibbous. This can feel like a betrayal. What was once good is turning sour and you must now be on guard.

The snake in your dream suggests there is a snake in your midst. Ishtar is telling you to look out for red flags regarding trust and loyalty.

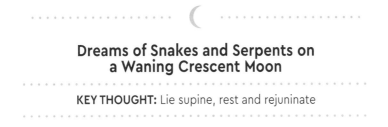

# Dreams of Snakes and Serpents on a Third Quarter Moon

**KEY THOUGHT:** Stick to the path

Dreams of snakes on the third quarter moon are powerful alignments of challenging metaphysical dynamics. The moon is in conflict as the tide of darkness reaches a point of overwhelming the light, while the forked tongue of the snake suggests that duplicity and cunning are at play.

Combined, this dream is Ishtar's clear warning that you must be hypervigilant in your dealings with others. The best way to avoid snakes is to steer clear of where they hide. Stick to the path, avoid the long grass and make sure you question everything. Just because it lies inactive doesn't mean it isn't dangerous.

# Dreams of Snakes and Serpents on a Waning Crescent Moon

**KEY THOUGHT:** Lie supine, rest and rejuninate

As the last vestige of light wraps around the shadowed waning crescent moon, a gorgeous arc of light graces the pre-dawn sky. This is a moment to reflect on your achievements in light and find peace with the coming shadow.

Ironically, as the moon approaches full shadow, the dawn approaches. What better time to shed the old moon and rejuvenate in time for the new moon and the new day?

Just as a snake would do, shedding your skin, acknowledging it for seeing you as far as it did and finding time to retreat, hibernate, rejuvenate and lie inactive is the message Ishtar is sending you in this dream.

# Spiders

Most of us know that arachnophobia is the fear of spiders. And the spiders' reputation of triggering panic is well earned. If we were to describe them as humans, we could be forgiven for confusing them with serial killers. They enter our homes uninvited. They are cunning, silent, ambitious and ruthless. They wait, sleepless in the dark, and move to strike with shocking speed. Spiders poison, sneak and play dirty, hiding, lurking and setting traps on the periphery until the unsuspecting wander into harm's way.

When an unfortunate victim gets caught, its end isn't swift – they get stuck in a web where panicking will only make matters worse. Their struggles to escape entangle them more and alert the predator that dinner is served. If this isn't terrifying enough, spiders don't immediately kill their prey; they paralyze their catch, wrap them in silk and keep them for later.

Knowing the anatomy, style and nature of spiders, it is no wonder that humans have a deep-rooted terror of what spiders represent. When we dream of spiders, we can use them to help us identify areas of fear, worry, anxiety and entrapment to avoid getting stuck.

## Dreams of Spiders on a New Moon

**KEY THOUGHT:** Where are you stuck?

While spiders represent negative emotions, you can use your dreams to steer your life with purpose and positivity. This is Ishtar's intention: she has your back and wants you to be aware of lurking dangers. Through spider dreams, you are being sent signals that you have fears and anxieties that are real, unresolved and perhaps hidden from the conscious life you would be well advised to address.

Dreams of spiders on the new moon give you an excellent opportunity to consider the root cause of the emotional upheaval. Are you stuck in a dead-end job or a poisonous relationship? What are you anxious about? What are you afraid of? How can you become unstuck?

You may fret for hours, days or even years over issues that feel like a chronic dark cloud over your head. Yet, if you pause and ask, "What's the worst that can happen?", this one question will either deal with the (non)issue by breaking the spell of fear it cast on you or start a healthy dialogue about what to do about the problem.

The healing can't start until you identify where you are stuck.

## Dreams of Spiders on a Waxing Crescent Moon

**KEY THOUGHT:** Tread carefully

The waxing crescent moon is a time in the lunar cycle when raw ideas are put into motion. This is a time to start work on creating the future you, the best you. Half the task of refining yourself is to add things you desire, and half is to remove things you don't. The latter is essential when thinking about the relevance of a dream involving spiders.

Spiders spin webs to snare their prey, and most of us have experienced times in life when we feel trapped. But remember, not all parts of the spider's web are sticky. If the spider treads carefully, it can navigate its web without difficulty.

As the moon begins to open up in its waxing crescent phase, it is still mostly dark; the place of shadow and fear. But just as the spider's web has safe paths, the moon, too, has light. If you tread carefully and think about what you are about to do, you can avoid getting trapped in arrangements that could consume your time, energy or happiness.

## Dreams of Spiders on a First Quarter Moon

**KEY THOUGHT:** Choose silk relationships

Since spiders set traps, they rarely engage in conflict. There is no struggle for them and their prey is either caught or not caught. This clear-cut, free-or-trapped scene conspires with the first quarter moon to create a time of opposites struggling for dominance.

When caught up in our daily lives, we rarely see the bigger picture of the complex web of relationships we weave. Just like spiders' webs, which are made of various types of silk – some sticky, some not – our social networks, too, are wildly diverse.

Some of your relationships may feel sticky, while others are silky smooth. It is Ishtar's desire that you don't simply avoid being snared but are also able to enjoy silky, luxurious connections. You must make a conscious choice to cut ties with ensnaring relations.

Remember that spiders don't just make webs with their silk. They also use silk to descend out of tricky or dangerous spots.

Whichever way you look at it, prioritizing silky relationships will serve you well.

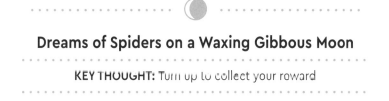

## Dreams of Spiders on a Waxing Gibbous Moon

**KEY THOUGHT:** Turn up to collect your reward

Spiders are masters of their craft: catching their desires. They know what they want, weave their plan and wait, and their patience is all part of their process. They don't walk away, nor do they get distracted. They have faith that the weaving of the web will manifest their desires.

And it does – all the spider needs to do is pick up the post.

Likewise, the waxing gibbous moon slowly glides toward full manifestation, being now mostly, but not entirely, illuminated. All that is left is a sliver of shadow.

Ishtar is directing your attention to endeavours that are now within reach. You should remember that just as the spider must collect and wrap up its gift in silk, you also must complete your tasks so that you can fully enjoy what you have been striving for.

There is a saying among athletes: "Medals are won in training. Competitions are just where you pick them up."

You have spun your web. You have revealed your desires and must turn up to collect the prize. Close the deal, dress the part, present ideas, whatever "turn up" means to you, and remember not to get complacent.

You must collect your reward.

## Dreams of Spiders on a Full Moon

**KEY THOUGHT:** Go about your business with tenacity and patience

There are few things more pristine than an immaculate, symmetrical spider's web glistening in the morning light, and there are few things more iconic as a symbol of neglect than cobwebs in a dusty attic. Yet these are the same thing, as spiders have their purpose.

The full moon is a time of full energy and completeness, yet it is also a time for the tide to turn, from waxing to waning. This moment can be energizing or anticlimactic, depending on your perspective. You can be confident that Ishtar is sending you positive messages, giving you the opportunity to appreciate achievements and dismiss the feeling of anticlimax (if it occurs), and go about your business with tenacity and patience, like a spider.

## Dreams of Spiders on a Waning Gibbous Moon

**KEY THOUGHT:** Rebuild and shine on, despite the setbacks

It is said that Robert the Bruce, the King of Scotland in the early 1300s, hid in a cave after a severe military defeat only to find renewed energy to fight again after watching a spider try to reweave its web. He could have found worse examples of focusing on the mission despite setbacks. Spiders are tenacious and unwavering in reorganizing their world when faced with disruption, and Ishtar thinks they are the perfect role model.

The waning moon has looming shadows in its midst – setbacks of light creeping across its face – yet it still shines bright and bold. Most people have had to deal with setbacks, shadows and the occasional disruption. The message contained in this dream is to rebuild and shine on, despite the setbacks.

## Dreams of Spiders on a Third Quarter Moon

**KEY THOUGHT:** Don't neglect the quiet corners of your life

Spiders not only represent threats to human wellbeing but also take advantage of neglect. Whether this is a fly that isn't paying attention and lands in its web or an attic where no one goes, the spider thrives, especially in the dark.

Yet while spiders can represent the stuff of nightmares, they are also very easily manageable. Paying attention, dusting unused rooms weekly and maintaining our affairs will keep them at bay. They hate the light.

The third quarter moon is an energetic and tense moment in the lunar calendar. It is a power play between light and shadow, between letting the predators in and keeping them at bay.

This dream is Ishtar's way of saying that you must be particularly vigilant – keep your eyes and the curtains open, let in the light, and don't neglect the quiet corners of your lives.

## Dreams of Spiders on a Waning Crescent Moon

**KEY THOUGHT:** Practice gratitude and send out positive vibrations

Spiders only know there is something trapped in their web by the vibrations caused by the struggle of the victim to free itself. It is counterintuitive to remain still in a situation when you are threatened, but sometimes playing dead, or at least not showing your hurt feelings, can be a camouflage against those that wish you ill.

The predatory spider in your dreams is representative of those who wish you harm and set traps for you. The waning crescent moon is the time in the lunar phase when shadow – threat, doubt, deceit – is dominant. Yet there is still a silver crescent – a silver lining – if you look close enough. If you can appreciate all the positive and stop struggling to illuminate what is lost in shadow, you can live in joy without sending out negative vibrations. Because when you struggle, the spiders will wake.

Practice gratitude and send out positive vibrations.

# Teeth

Using a single word, dreams of teeth represent power, and, similarly, dreams of losing teeth mean the loss of power.

Teeth are only visible in nature or in our culture on a handful of occasions, and these each empower us in their own way. From an evolutionary standpoint, most animals that have ever presented a threat to our survival have been a threat because of their bite: their teeth. If we were to be in serious conflict with another, biting would be an aggressive option for us to use. To bite or to be bitten is a power play.

From a cultural perspective (and ironically, almost polar opposite to the message contained in biting), our smile is very close in its action to when we bare our teeth in anger. Yet what smiles communicate couldn't be more different from biting. Smiling and laughing are inviting, attractive and endearing actions that contain much power in their own way. While we may be less likely to be bitten by a lion these days, being shunned and shut out by society would cause emotional trauma. Our social appeal relies on our attractiveness, and smiling is a significant part of our presentation.

Perhaps the most powerful tool we humans possess is our voice; in modern culture, our assertiveness – our "bark" – is our new bite.

There is power in your bark, your bite and your beauty, and losing your teeth would compromise them all.

There are historical, cultural and spiritual connections with teeth that support these ideas. Many ancient cultures – the Babylonians, for one – collected and wore as jewellery the teeth of animals. Dental care was a critical spiritual practice, and they perceived teeth as tears, suggesting the dreamer would soon experience challenging times regarding communication. The Mesopotamians associated the loss of teeth with a loss of inner guidance and focus – a loss of communication with our intuition.

## Dreams of Teeth on a New Moon

**KEY THOUGHT:** Consider where in life you desire more control

When you consider dreams of teeth, you must consider your relationship with power (or a lack of power) if you are to glean meaning from the message. The dream on the new moon provides an exciting opportunity to review where you may have, lack or want power.

The new moon is a time for reinvention, reviewing an unsatisfying status quo or drafting new ideas. So, dreams of teeth – dreams of *power* – at this moment are a prompt to take a personal audit and get a sense for where in life you feel powerless or desire greater influence.

You don't need to take any action. This dream isn't a call to arms; it is a call to *awareness*. This desire for more power doesn't need to be a sinister play for dominance. There is no shame in seeking control over your bad habits, wishing to be heard in your place of work or bolstering your self-esteem if you are in a challenging personal relationship.

Dreams of teeth on the new moon prompt you to consider where in life you may wish to manifest greater control over your situation.

## Dreams of Teeth on a Waxing Crescent Moon

**KEY THOUGHT:** Set achievable goals to reclaim your voice

The crescent moon is a time to start new ideas, and this can be incredibly empowering. It isn't insignificant to have a dream of teeth during this lunar phase. For Ishtar, teeth are a metaphor for power and control in your life, so, in effect, she is doubling down, and you should take note.

Following a dream of teeth on the waxing crescent moon, you have a clear calling to take steps toward reclaiming ownership of a feature of your life that you have perhaps let slip. Identify any area of your life where you have become complacent or have given away your ownership. Then decide to reclaim it and take a step toward that objective.

If this is personal health, take a ten-minute walk. If this is finances, choose a single item on the budget that you can live without. If this is the dynamics of a relationship, find a single moment to say, "No, I would prefer . . .", and use your voice to start to rebuild your stance.

Choose one area where power is lacking and choose something you can do to start reclaiming your power – all achievable goals.

## Dreams of Teeth on a First Quarter Moon

**KEY THOUGHT:** Ask why you let others make decisions for you

With power comes responsibility. While this sounds nice in theory, sometimes you may just want someone else to decide for you, and that's okay.

If you dream of teeth on the first quarter moon, you have a clear message from Ishtar that you have choices in life. You may want to make some choices for yourself, whereas you may wish other people would make some choices. There are also the choices you simply don't care about. This dream is about identifying which choice falls into which category.

If you wish to choose for yourself, you must ensure that you voice your opinion. This may or may not win the argument, but without speaking up you give away your power without making any effort.

If you don't care about the choices, this isn't the time to flex power just for the sake of it. There is grace in saying that you are flexible and are happy to defer.

The most interesting category – the area where most power can be reclaimed – is when you want someone to choose for you even if you have a preference. This is probably the area Ishtar is most concerned about, as it is clearly a willful act to concede your power and therefore your self-esteem.

Dreams of teeth on the first quarter moon provide a clear message to examine where you give away your power and compromise yourself when doing so. If you can identify when you do this, you can then ask yourself why.

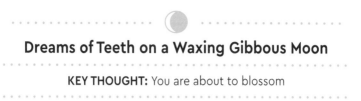

## Dreams of Teeth on a Waxing Gibbous Moon

**KEY THOUGHT:** You are about to blossom

Ishtar's primary message during the waxing gibbous moon is to finalize details and complete the picture. With dreams of teeth representing power, assertiveness, social appeal and strength of opinion, you have an excellent opportunity to recognize areas in your life where you are growing to maturity, metaphorically allowing your adult teeth to replace your milk teeth.

Whether developing communication skills or meditating on finding more peace and self-assurance in our daily lives, most of us strive to build strength in areas that are important to us. The message in this dream is that you are headed in the right direction and that your efforts will soon pay off.

Stay the course with efforts for self-improvement as you blossom.

## Dreams of Teeth on a Full Moon

**KEY THOUGHT:** Express your character with joy and confidence

A magnificent alignment of forces is at play when you experience dreams of teeth on the full moon. It is no mere coincidence that werewolves are said to howl at this time in the lunar cycle. Dreams of teeth are messages from Ishtar that you need to examine where you have and lack power. The full moon is the most powerful phase when power is on display.

This isn't a time to assert your power; it is a time to accept what is and what isn't. Sure, there is power in standing and saying, "I am . . .", but there is also power in saying, "I know that I am not . . ." Having the strength to recognize and verbalize what isn't your strength displays just as much confidence as having the strength to recognize and verbalize what is.

Dreams of teeth on the full moon tell you to accept your character for what it is, celebrate it and express it with joy and confidence.

## Dreams of Teeth on a Waning Gibbous Moon

**KEY THOUGHT:** Delegate

The waning gibbous moon literally means "declining shape". This phase of the lunar cycle represents the beginning of the retreat from full expression to closure and renewal. Dreams of teeth during this phase contain messages that while you can celebrate areas in your life where you are capable of displaying confidence, you weren't designed to be good at everything.

In some areas of internal corporate messaging, admitting weakness is . . . a weakness. "Areas of opportunity" and "potential for growth" have their place, but can be exhausting. Indeed, ask any gardener how to get the best out of their plants, and they may well include pruning as a potent technique. More decisively, pulling out problems, weeds and bad teeth by their roots is the surest way to rid yourself of trouble.

Delegating, giving others a chance to lead or simply letting go of root causes of concern, can do wonders for your soul, and dreams of teeth on the waning gibbous moon encourage you to delegate to lighten your burden.

## Dreams of Teeth on a Third Quarter Moon

**KEY THOUGHT:** It's time to detox

The third quarter moon is a time of transition, when choices are required. Now is an important time to step up and make big decisions, and more specifically some big "no" decisions: it is time to edit. Likewise, dreams of teeth are Ishtar's way of making you aware of areas in your psyche that desire more "say".

This dream at this point in the lunar calendar couldn't be a more explicit message. It is not simply about trimming the unwanted from your life, but also about focusing these decisions on areas that are most corrosive to your self-esteem.

Toxic relationships, toxic workplaces and toxic mindsets all undermine your power. While it may be terrifying to think of leaving a situation that is at least stable, you will know deep down that you are kidding yourself if you believe tolerating a bad situation for fear of upheaval is a good long-term strategy.

It is time to bite the bullet, rip off the Band-Aid and detox.

## Dreams of Teeth on a Waning Crescent Moon

**KEY THOUGHT:** Nurture others

Dreams of teeth on the waning crescent moon are messages from Ishtar to finalize ways to hand off control to others.

While you may want to ensure that you are in control of things in your circle of concern, you may also want to avoid doing tasks that drain your psyche and aren't the best use of your energy. You won't want your kids to trip, yet you also probably don't want to be tying their shoelaces for the rest of their lives. Likewise, dreams of teeth on the waning crescent moon contain messages that you can nurture others to take responsibility for themselves.

This nurturing of others is a powerful act that can expand your circle of responsibilities while reducing your burden. By fine-tuning your guidance of others in the ways you want things done, you can extend your reach and power to create your best life.

# Time, Clocks and Watches

What even *is* time? It's infinite, yet there never seems to be enough of it. It appears to move at different speeds depending on our emotions. How do we know it existed before we began to track it? Is it universal or manmade? At the end of the day, time is a mystery.

I love the analogy that each day is like a suitcase. On some days, we seem able to fit more in than others. Einstein famously said that the only reason for time was to prevent everything from happening at once. I also love the idea of likening a day to a jar. First, we fill it with stones – the big, important things – until there's no more room in the jar. Then we top it up with gravel – smaller, less important things – until there's no more room. Then we top it up with sand – the trivial stuff – until there's no more room. And even after that, there is still room – time – to pour in a beer or a glass of wine. No matter how much we fill our day, there is always more we can do.

The point is; the need to manage time is a very human condition and not one we seem at peace with. Unlike the rest of the animal and plant kingdoms, humankind felt compelled to calibrate it. First, with sundials, and later with clocks and watches, we devised ways to measure and convey time in a structured, predictable, conventional manner. And since then, we have struggled to manage it – or manage ourselves within that structure. Expressed this way, the idea of time does appear to be a classic manmade folly; ever since we devised it, we have been up against it.

Many of us have overslept at some point in our life, waking to see that we are late for something important to us. That jolt of panic we experience when we realize we are late is a primal panic, even though this foe is ethereal and not what our DNA evolved for us to handle. Most of us have been late for flights, stuck in traffic, or have simply lost track of time and have suffered as a consequence of the mismanagement of time. And this suffering is so widespread and upsetting that it has made its way into our subconscious.

In many ways, the human mind has out-evolved our bodies and our limbic system. Only a few hundred thousand years after we climbed out of the trees, humans have constructed a temporal framework upon which we hang our civilization, minute by minute. Time is the master of our age. It chases us. It rushes us. It will always catch up with us. It will steal our opportunities, our youth, and our beauty.

Yet it also gives us wisdom, children, gardens, seasons, inner calm, meditation, answers, and the healing of wounds – of the flesh and of the heart.

Dreams of time – of watches, clocks, being late or being early – are some of the most common dreams we experience; they are a potent sign from Ishtar that we have concerns about the future and stress regarding the management of our daily lives.

## Dreams of Time, Clocks and Watches on a New Moon

**KEY THOUGHT:** Prepare

When we dream of time on the new moon, we have a unique opportunity to identify some of our core subconscious stressors and make meaningful changes in how we manage our lives.

Dreams of time – being late, early, watching the clock, etc. – are like canaries in the coal mine of our daily toil; signs that we are in danger of mismanaging our work/life balance, unaware of the toxins we are breathing. Whether it's dreaming of being late for school, work, our wedding, or any form of deadline, Ishtar is telling us that we are stressed about our environment and should do something about that.

And there can be a few different reasons for this stress. Apart from the obvious fear of missing opportunities, we should also take a moment to examine our preparedness. Being prepared is perhaps the greatest antidote to anxiety. To paraphrase a common proverb, a stitch in time saves ... umm, ... *time*.

With the new moon comes new opportunities, ideas, endeavours, and mindsets. With dreams of time on the new moon, Ishtar is prompting us to be more aware of how we manage our endeavours to avoid stressing our unconscious selves. And the best way to do that is to be prepared. The confidence we gain from being prepared will transform the experiences we have... every time.

## Dreams of Time, Clocks and Watches on a Waxing Crescent Moon

**KEY THOUGHT:** Be kind to yourself in your planning

As the waxing crescent moon reveals its nascent form, likewise, our subconscious mind ruminates on the things in life that are at the beginning of their life journey. Relationships in their earliest stages, new projects and new jobs are all fair game for Ishtar to reflect on.

Dreams about time present an interesting revelation about how we manage – or *think* we manage – our lives. These dreams suggest that deep down, we may lack confidence that we have enough resources, information, support, etc. – to complete the task within the allotted parameters – time, budget, etc.

There are two ways we can reconcile this equation. One would be to address our resources, and the other would be to ask if the allotted parameters are realistic, fair, or even necessary.

When we dream of time on the waxing crescent moon, Ishtar is informing our conscious mind that when we embark on new adventures, we are kind to ourselves in our planning.

## Dreams of Time, Clocks and Watches on a First Quarter Moon

**KEY THOUGHT:** Consider your bigger dilemmas, weigh the pros and cons, and move in a healthy direction.

Dreams of time on the first quarter moon are critical messages from Ishtar that decisions should be made about the feasibility of some aspects of our endeavours.

Classically, dreams about time are dreams about resources – time, support, willpower or even confidence. And dreams on the first quarter moon, when the moon is split in two, can inform us that we, too, might be wrestling with which way to go.

Just like when we cross a busy street or overtake a vehicle, there are times when we must decide whether we have the space we need. These are very visceral examples of decision-making. Most things in life are less immediate, but that does not mean indecision won't eat at us. We do not want to stand at the curb forever. Nor do we wish to put ourselves in danger. On a subconscious level, this dilemma stays hidden.

Should we marry him, should we *leave* him, should we ask for a pay rise, should we ...? These are questions we could probably answer quite quickly if asked. The problem is; when in our daily life do we have the emotional space to reflect on such things?

That's where Ishtar can help.

Dreams of time on the first quarter moon are her way of prompting us to consider the bigger dilemmas in our life, weigh the pros and cons, and move in a healthy direction.

## Dreams of Time, Clocks and Watches
## on a Waxing Gibbous Moon

**KEY THOUGHT:** Do away with the devil of stress
by letting go of its hold on you

When the waxing gibbous moon graces the night sky, it bathes us in ideas that are near to completion, requiring only the final touches, the details. And when we dream of time, Ishtar is alerting us to the subconscious anxieties we feel about our endeavours in life.

It would benefit us to recognize that clocks are manmade, and the stress we feel from delivering our work within such artificial confines might be a good motivator, but we should not compromise quality if quality is, indeed, the priority. Nor should it compromise our health.

Clocks, watches, and the structure of time can be our friends. They can also be our enemy. When we take our time baking a cake but are rushed when applying the icing, is the end result desirable? The devil is in the details. Or, more accurately, the devil is the guy telling us we don't have the time to attend to the finishing touches.

And just like time, the devil is a state of mind.

Dreams of time in the waxing gibbous moon are Ishtar's way of drawing our attention to the details and either doing away with them or doing away with the thing that compromises their being done well. Either way, we do away with the devil of stress by letting go of its hold on us.

# Dreams of Time, Clocks and Watches on a Full Moon

**KEY THOUGHT:** Make time for your own standards, and don't waste time worrying about the opinion of others

The full moon's climax of illumination matches perfectly with the anticlimax that what was ascendant has peaked and will begin its decline. It is a moment of high energy and mixed emotions; a good time to reflect on our achievements. Its light will illuminate, its zenith will provide context and, hopefully, the lunar cycle will provide perspective.

When we dream of time, we are accessing the anxieties that swim beneath our awareness and feed off the unresolved tensions and unmet expectations. Warren Buffet is rumoured to have said, when asked about the secret to good financial investment, that it was the same as the secret to a good marriage: low expectations. While that may sound depressing, he has a point. How much more enjoyable is an art project when done for its own sake, without the pressure of expectations?

We cannot be hurt by the disapproval of others if we don't strive solely to meet their approval: to meet their expectations. If, instead, we strive for our own quality and do our best to achieve that, we make ourselves immune to the hostile environment of the expectations of others, especially if we allow ourselves to be defined in part by their approval.

We should set our expectations high. We should make time for our own standards and not waste time worrying about the opinion of others.

# Dreams of Time, Clocks and Watches on a Waning Gibbous Moon

**KEY THOUGHT:** Good, fast, cheap; pick two

There is an inherent sense of foreboding during the waning phase of the lunar cycle, of dimming light, the coming shadow, and of loss of the complete. But the waning phase can, and *should*, be seen not as a death but as a consolidation of what is valued and of journeying toward resolution.

When we dream of time, we open ourselves to accessing insight into how we manage our lives, resources, time and emotions when we must work within restrictive parameters, rules and regulations.

When we dream of time on the waning gibbous moon, Ishtar calls to our attention that there are opportunities for us to navigate life's challenges more flexibly. Because it's not the project's quality or efficiency that causes us stress, nor is it the clock; it's our interpretation of the relationship between the three.

There is an expression in manufacturing that sums it up perfectly: "Good, fast, cheap; pick two." If we were to desire good, fast *and* cheap, we would generate tension, but let go of one, and the rest is easy. And this is Ishtar's message when we dream of time on the waning gibbous moon: Good, fast, cheap; pick two.

# Dreams of Time, Clocks and Watches on a Third Quarter Moon

**KEY THOUGHT:** Reassess your assumptions to see if they are still relevant

The sibling of the first quarter moon, the third quarter phase, heralds a time of tension, split personality and indecision. Yet it can also prepare us to clear the way for new, fresher ideas. As we delve deeper into the waning phase, we must accept that it's time to wrap things up.

I have fond childhood memories of playing outside in the summer months until the skies went dark and the streetlights began to illuminate. I dreaded the moment that the parents would call us all in and know that it was imminent. Yet dread was the wrong emotion. I knew that, once in, a warm drink and a bath would be waiting, and I loved them both. Transitions often feel worse than that to which we transition. Dreams on the third quarter remind us that only once we finish a chapter can we start a new one.

Dreams of time are projections of subconscious anxiety about conforming and adhering to constraints that may or may not be relevant. Reassessing the relevance of the assumptions we make (such as wanting to play outside even when it's dark), and deciding if they still serve us or if we are ready to move on, can make all the difference between a good transition and a painful one.

## Dreams of Time, Clocks and Watches on a Waning Crescent Moon

**KEY THOUGHT:** Resolve the unresolved in a positive way

The waning crescent moon is a phase I find particularly beautiful, as it hints at form and is visible in the morning sky just before dawn. It is an early riser yet is the swansong of the lunar cycle. Soon, the sun will rise, and soon after that, the new moon will begin a new cycle. It holds a special place in the heavens and is an inspiration for us to settle the unresolved.

When we dream of time, clocks, watches, or any other restrictive construct, our subconscious is projecting anxiety about limited resources into our awareness. This stress, to complete what we had assumed we would be able to, can be apparent or subliminal, but it is always harmful. If we cannot do what we had intended or assumed we would, next best would be to frame our mindset so as not to cause ourselves undue anxiety and harm.

Sometimes, when I write until late, I might stress that I have hours of work in front of me. In moments of clarity, I might realize that what might take a tired mind two hours to do at night would take a fresh, rested mind only 30 minutes to do the following morning. While the work may not be completed, the work*flow is*. Within that decision, there is resolution and positive emotion.

When we dream of time on the waning crescent moon, we are challenged by Ishtar to see the situation for what it is and resolve the workflow in a way that feels right. When we use phrases like; on hold, between jobs, taking a sabbatical, considering options, etc., we resolve the unresolved in a positive way and avoid letting unfinished business gnaw at us. Better still, if we add a reminder in our calendar to pick up the project at a later date, we no longer even have to think about it.

# Tornadoes, Storms and Bad Weather

Tornadoes and other types of stormy weather can be mesmerizing. They snake from Father Sky, crowned with storm clouds that rage with thunder and lightning, down to Mother Earth with a violence that is impossible to comprehend and a beauty that is impossible to ignore.

Destructive forces of nature are more alien to us than . . . well, aliens! Without sentience, they are not even cold-hearted; they have no heart at all. They are unpredictable, and we can do nothing to prevent them. At best, we can avoid or outrun them, but there is no negotiation. They will tear up anything we create, from cars to buildings, animals and entire neighbourhoods. Then, vanishing literally into thin air, they leave no trace of their existence, only the destruction in their wake. And while this chapter mentions tornadoes specifically, its interpretations apply to all forms of tempest from the skies.

All forces of nature have the power and potential for random destruction planted in our psyches. But where tornadoes, hurricanes and even common lightning storms differ from, say, earthquakes or floods is in their beauty. In the American Midwest's "Tornado Alley", a community of "storm chasers" makes it their business to pursue all the tornadoes they can find, so strong is their lure. These monsters from the sky are deeply ingrained in popular culture, from Dorothy's dream in *The Wizard of Oz* and cable TV specials on storm chasers to tragic almost-weekly news stories during tornado season. No wonder our subconscious is so fascinated by them.

But as usual with Ishtar, she always has good news and important information, and the opportunities to deepen your self-awareness are plentiful if you can accurately interpret the message she is sending you in your dream.

## Dreams of Tornadoes on a New Moon

**KEY THOUGHT:** What if you could wipe the slate clean?

Tornadoes bring chaos, and dreams of tornadoes warn of the same. Yet the timing of this dream provides valuable insight and context for the subconscious fears you are expressing.

The new moon is a time of rebirth, renewal and creative thinking. More often than not, a painter would prefer a blank canvas to a messy one, and it would be nice to think of life in the same way. Yet life is chaotic, busy and nonstop. Rarely do you have the opportunity to start afresh. Even original thinking is virtually impossible when you carry the emotional baggage of a life well lived.

The destructive force of the tornado in your dream may instinctively evoke terror and panic. Yet, if you look at what is in danger of destruction – things that are well established – you can see that you can glean alternative interpretations from your dream.

How great would it be to start again, move to a different part of the country, take a road trip, have the chance to replace your wardrobe all in one go, or get a new computer with no files or folders slowing down the hard drive. That is what Ishtar is suggesting that you consider when you dream of tornadoes; what if you could wipe the slate clean?

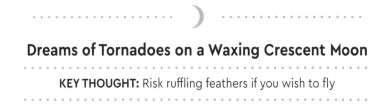

## Dreams of Tornadoes on a Waxing Crescent Moon

**KEY THOUGHT:** Risk ruffling feathers if you wish to fly

Just as tornadoes curve from sky to earth as they begin their path of devastation, the waxing crescent moon curves in elegant, nascent light as it begins its journey to illumination. Similar in form yet opposite in tone, dreams of tornadoes on the waxing crescent moon are a powerful signal of the start of a significant life journey.

Whether this is a relationship, a job or any other change in direction, most of us know what our "should", "woulds" and "coulds" are, but we allow ourselves to be talked out of pursuing them by "ifs" and "buts".

Take inspiration from the moon's persistence. Waxing crescents, like ebbing tides, are desires for progress that don't let shadow or land mass deter them – the moon will become full and the tide will reach its height. The tornado is also determined to fulfil its purpose; to bridge sky and earth, even though it understands that not all will approve of its dance.

If you persist, you, too, will achieve your goals. It is impossible to leave no footprints as you pursue your desires. While you certainly won't wish harm on others, if you are afraid to place the inconvenience of others above your own, you risk losing control of your destiny – husks to be blown every which way by the winds of others.

Dreams of tornadoes on the waxing crescent moon are Ishtar's way of saying that you must risk ruffling feathers if you wish to fly.

## Dreams of Tornadoes on a First Quarter Moon

**KEY THOUGHT:** Remain objective and proceed with courage

One of the most fascinating things about a tornado's destructive power is its focus. Often, aerial footage of the aftermath of a tornado can reveal an almost knife-like cut through fields and, tragically, neighbourhoods. While the proximity of a tornado is still subject to high winds and debris, the intense walls of the funnel can leave one house standing while it razes its neighbour to the ground leaving only its basement in place.

Dreams of tornadoes on the first quarter moon are signs of decision and indecision, light and dark, control and loss of control, security and ruin, and are about the delicate knife-edge you walk between the two sides of this equation. You won't want to be too vulnerable, exposing yourself to unnecessary dangers. Yet, by hiding in the basement of life, you may miss the beauty, light and adventure it offers.

Ishtar presents both danger and security – light and dark – in your dream, encouraging you to walk the line between the two. You must trust in your decisions and accept the consequences that may come. You must remain objective and proceed with courage.

## Dreams of Tornadoes on a Waxing Gibbous Moon

**KEY THOUGHT:** Ask others for support

With only a sliver of the moon remaining in shadow and the majority illuminated in the sun's light, this phase of the lunar cycle is joyful in its optimism even as work still needs to be done.

Dreams of tornadoes at any time of the moon's cycle represent the potential for chaos, ruin and fear. It is especially potent during the waxing crescent as there is so much to lose if you drop the ball now.

Just as building a house of cards or a game of Jenga becomes more fraught with anxiety as each reaches a new level, many of your plans can be scattered to the winds if you don't nail them down, make them watertight and secure them.

Now is a time to consider the opportunities you are pursuing and ensure these are not damaged by unexpected turbulence. Most often, it is friends and family that can offer the best support, and we shouldn't be afraid to ask if we need it.

## Dreams of Tornadoes on a Full Moon

**KEY THOUGHT:** It is what you do in the eye of the
storm that will set you apart from others

The illumination of the moon, and therefore its power, is at its peak when it is full. The destructive power of a tornado is at its peak when it is on the ground, ripping circles in the earth as it spins at terrifying speed.

After a peak, there will be a decline. The moon will drift further into shadow and the tornado will pass. Yet, within this peak time is a distinct moment of reflection – the eye of the storm – when you can be still, objectively observe all the chaos and meditate on your place in life.

Ishtar is telling you that while you may be swept along in many aspects of your life or be thrown the debris of everyday living from all directions, you have an opportunity to find a moment amid the chaos to reclaim control.

You may not have the power to control the weather or even other people; you only have the power to control yourself, your actions and your thoughts. You may feel panicked from time to time; this is a given. It is what you choose to do in the eye of the storm that will set you apart from others.

## Dreams of Tornadoes on a Waning Gibbous Moon

**KEY THOUGHT:** Batten down the hatches

As the moon enters its waning phase, shadows and negativity are on the rise. It is a good strategy to prioritize *in*surance over *a*ssurance and consolidate your gains against inclement weather.

With dreams of tornadoes, their prevailing winds promise to bring chaos and ruin to anyone who is either unprepared for it, unaware of it or unwilling to take action to avoid it.

In life pursuits, there are creative phases, productive phases, reflective phases, and then there is maintenance. Any sailor will be familiar with the expression "Batten down the hatches". This is a direction to prepare for stormy weather by securing vulnerabilities.

## Dreams of Tornadoes on a Third Quarter Moon

**KEY THOUGHT:** Seek shelter

Most of us have friends or acquaintances that bring calm to our day, and maybe some of us have friends, colleagues or family members who are more dynamic than others. While you may not enjoy the downsides to some relationships, their highs may bring you enough entertainment, income or any other types of valued life experience to keep you "in exchange". These relationships are profitable.

The unprofitable ones take more from the potluck dinner than they contribute. Unfortunately, if you have such relationships in your lives, these may be complex and . . . well, stormy.

Dreams of tornadoes on the third quarter moon mirror similar dreams on the first quarter moon, but while both dreams are messages about light and dark, they differ in one important way. In the waning phase of the lunar cycle, the third quarter moon concerns itself more with resolution and the coming of shadow. As such, Ishtar's message in this dream is to seek shelter. Whatever storms are in your life will happen whether you like them or not. Standing and watching, wondering what may happen, only plays into the tornado's desire to disrupt. If this is what you want, you don't need to take action. But if this isn't what you want, your dream is advising you to take evasive action.

Chaos is headed your way and you should seek shelter. This could take the form of avoidance, support from friends, meditation or more sleep. Only you can know the challenges you face and the armour you need.

## Dreams of Tornadoes on a Waning Crescent Moon

**KEY THOUGHT:** Separate the things that
soothe us from the things that chafe

Shadow has now almost completely overpowered the moon, leaving only a thin curve of light. Dreams at this time on the lunar cycle are reminders to tie loose ends so you can close out life's present chapter in peace.

All this may be disrupted, of course. Tempest and chaos can descend from the sky without warning and spoil what was otherwise a lovely picnic. If that happens, your plans can be left in tatters, scattered to the winds, ruined or lost. In your dreams, the looming destruction may not be all bad.

During agricultural harvesting, separating the wheat from the chaff – the wanted from the unwanted – involves throwing the harvest to the winds. Anything that is bad catches the wind and is blown away; anything that is good is returned.

Dreams of tornadoes on the waning crescent moon are a clear message from Ishtar that you would benefit from taking a personal inventory of your friends, activities, assets and time investments and separating the things that soothe you from the things that chafe.

# Water

Wherever there is water, there is life, and as surely as water is indestructible, life is irrepressible. Not just the barest of life; emotions, too, are part of this profound ecosystem. Tears of joy and sadness are the outpourings of emotion.

Dreams of water are dreams of emotions. Flowing, blocked, clear, murky, calm, stormy, refreshing or frightening – where there are dreams of water, there are warnings from Ishtar of your emotional undercurrent. A river runs through you as you course through time. As surely as the banks of a river pass you as you float downstream, your emotions pass you as you flow through life: an unending stream of swirls and rapids and tranquil turns. As the tide ebbs and flows, so does your joy. Once you accept this and can see your emotions as passing moments, you can navigate life with daring confidence. You drink it, swim, clean, play in it, water your gardens, sing in the rain, ride the waves and fall asleep to its soothing rhythm.

Earth is the only planet we know of that contains water, and the only planet that supports life. Even *on* this planet, with oceans covering 70 per cent of its surface, there is life *only* where there is water. Anyone who has flown over continents may have looked down to see vast expanses of land with little activity compared to small, concentrated areas of activity – from the Nile Delta to the watering holes of the Serengeti, the evidence is overwhelming.

We also fear water and, in the age of science, we can only wonder at its unimaginable depth and mystery. There are few fates that induce more anxiety than succumbing to water's fury.

Water is such an essential component of life that it was created on the very first day. We have had water on the brain since *before* we had brains. Its primal chemistry and shape-shifting purity is the nectar of everything humans love: fertility, creativity and wellbeing. It is the indestructible source of all sentience – feelings and emotions.

Yet, there is one thing that has power over water: the moon.

## Dreams of Water on a New Moon

**KEY THOUGHT:** Your life will only flourish where you water it

Dreams of water during the new moon lunar phase are profound evocations from Ishtar, suggesting a perfect alignment of powerful creative forces. In the context of dream interpretation, the new moon represents a fresh start or a blank canvas: an empty cup. It is a time of creativity – to manifest your desires – limited only by your imagination. It is a time to remind yourself that you can fill your cup with whatever you want.

Likewise, dreams of water are cleansing, playful, fertile messages that life abounds. You water your garden, quench your thirst and dance for rain, and when you do, the fruits of your efforts feel like gifts from the universe. Dreams of water are the same: messages from Ishtar to water your ideas, quench your thirst for life and dance for joy.

Even hostile waters, such as tsunamis, floods and storms, wash away the unwanted. From Noah's Ark to spring showers, fresh ideas require fresh water to cleanse and grow. And just as your garden will only flourish where you water it, the same goes for life.

## Dreams of Water on a Waxing Crescent Moon

**KEY THOUGHT:** Breach the sands of inertia and allow life to flow

One of my favourite YouTube videos is of a beach sand bar almost breached by a rising fresh-water lake behind it. Some children playing in the sand dig a tiny channel through the sand, from the lake to the ocean. There is a beautiful moment when the lake begins to trickle into their channel, and when that happens, everyone watching knows the inevitable: once the flow begins, the forces of nature will do the rest.

The trickle of water washes away a little sand, allowing more water through the channel. This, in turn, washes away a little more sand, and so on. In a matter of minutes, the trickle the children innocently started develops into a raging torrent 20 metres wide that completely empties the lake. And all it took was a couple of children with plastic spades.

Dreams of water on the waxing crescent moon are messages from Ishtar that if you can overcome the levees of fear and pessimism, you can release a flow of energy capable of changing the world.

It doesn't matter the size of the breach; what matters is that you breach it enough, as those children did with their spades, to allow life, inspiration and creativity to flow. After that, the forces of nature will do the rest.

## Dreams of Water on a First Quarter Moon

**KEY THOUGHT:** Act with decisive energy
when the right wave comes your way

Our ancestors waited for the third quarter moon to use moonlight to purify water for spiritual rituals and ceremonies. For millennia, water dreams on this moon phase have been particularly valued and offer powerful lessons in patience.

One personal example that springs to mind is from my childhood, when my grandfather took me boating. After playing for some time, way out in the breakers, we became stuck on a sand bar. While I became scared, my grandfather remained calm, explaining that the tide was low and that when it rose again, so would we. And he was right. I have always believed, in times of concern, that the tide will turn.

On a different note, I have been blessed on several occasions to be invited to teach at a few retreats, some of which were in tropical locations. Often, these exotic retreats included surf lessons as a metaphor to connect with nature – to work with it, not *against* it. Surfing wasn't really my thing, but they have a point.

The art of "catching a wave" involves a few key decisions that must align. Positioning just where the waves begin to break is essential, and then it is a waiting game until luck delivers a crest right where you are. At this point, you must either let it pass or paddle like crazy to "catch" it. The choice to paddle, the timing of the choice and your commitment to the effort must be instant, synchronous and wholehearted. If you hold back for even a fraction of a second, the wave will pass you, it will be too late and you would be better off conserving energy and letting it pass.

Successful surfers let 50 waves pass for every wave they try to catch. What makes them successful is that when they see the right opportunity, their decision to commit is instant, synchronous and wholehearted. As a result, they expend the least energy and enjoy the biggest successes.

Dreams of water on the first quarter moon are Ishtar's way of communicating that you can be more successful with less effort if you choose your opportunities with more discretion and act with decisive energy when the right wave comes your way.

## Dreams of Water on a Waxing Gibbous Moon

**KEY THOUGHT:** Be mindful of the gardens of love you nurture

Dreams of water on the waxing gibbous pertain to the fine detail of your life. Full disclosure: I am not a very good gardener, as my house plants often remind me. While I don't have green fingers, they do get green with envy when I see how much healthier my friends' plants seem to fare. Apparently, the secret is in the watering.

Where there is no water, there is no life. Yet *too much* water can be a terrible force of destruction, so even overwatering some flowers can spoil them. Flowers that grow in the dirt are not my specialty, but the flowers of the universe, the soul and the mind are more of the kind I have had success caring for. Nevertheless, the principles for their care are the same; some flowers require more tending to than others.

Dreams of water on the waning crescent moon are calls from Ishtar for you to be mindful of the gardens of love you nurture. You must love each flower as it needs to be loved.

## Dreams of Water on a Full Moon

**KEY THOUGHT:** Seek spiritual balance and
reflect that in everything you do

There is perhaps no more classic image of tranquillity and natural beauty than that of the full moon, low above the ocean's horizon, reflected as a shimmering silver path upon the smooth mercurial surface of the water.

In the context of dream interpretation, however, there is a contradiction here, and dreams of water on the full moon are interesting for that reason. The full moon in this image is fully revealed, high energy, visible and heaven bound. The water is the opposite: dark, tranquil, mysterious and earth bound. Dreams of water on the full moon represent all these things – in balance. These are a celebration of body and spirit, water and air, the formed and the formless, passion and reason, the feminine and the masculine.

Dreams of water on the full moon are a call from Ishtar to seek spiritual balance and reflect that in everything you do.

## Dreams of Water on a Waning Gibbous Moon

**KEY THOUGHT:** Carry an umbrella in case it rains

As the shadows begin to creep over the moon, the waning gibbous moon forewarns that you should start preparing for doubt and the darkening of your spiritual skies.

There are many signs in nature that when read correctly could provide important information for your wellbeing. Many people can tell when storms were coming just by the way their joints feel, and most people have experienced the close humidity that precedes summer thunderstorms. Perhaps the eeriest of these examples are the stories of wild animals heading for the hills as the Indian ocean receded far from the beaches of Indonesia just before the 2004 Boxing Day tsunami.

Dreams of water on the waning gibbous moon are Ishtar's gentle way of suggesting that while unsettling things may be headed your way, there are simple, common-sense actions you can take to guard against harm.

Carrying an umbrella in case it rains is the surest way to ensure you don't get caught by surprise.

## Dreams of Water on a Third Quarter Moon

KEY THOUGHT: Planning will ground us,
while indecision will wash us away

There is a tidal island on the border of the northern French coastal regions of Brittany and Normandy called Mont Saint-Michel that hosts a spectacular abbey. Its architectural beauty aside, the added peculiarity of this gorgeous site is that it is accessible by footpath at low tide, but not at high tide. Any family that has visited this special place will know that when it is time to go, it really is time to go. If they delay for ten minutes and let the tide get ahead of them, they should plan on staying the night. But worse, if they delay for only *five* minutes before starting to walk back, they may only make it halfway before they are caught up in rising waters and up to their necks in problems.

Like at Mont Saint-Michel, dreams of water on the third quarter moon. are telling you that when you choose to leave an island – such as a job or a relationship – you must plan to exit at low tide, when you are most secure. Financial planning, support networks and mental health will keep you grounded, while indecision will wash you away.

## Dreams of Water on a Waning Crescent

**KEY THOUGHT:** Find an emotional safe harbour until the skies clear

No matter how rugged a ship and its crew may be, if cruel winds, stormy waters or life's unpredictable undercurrent become overwhelming, it will seek safe harbour.

Dreams of water on the waning crescent moon are Ishtar's calling to ensure that you are aware of your options. There may be times when you can resolve your challenges. Riding out the storm – facing your challenges – is always best done when you are emotionally anchored. But what if you are not?

If you are feeling unmoored, adrift or in the doldrums, there may be no resolution available at that moment, but you can still stay healthy and dry.

Safe harbours are places where you know you are secure from inclement circumstances. Friends, loved ones, meditation, journals, walking and, for some, swimming are all healthy ways to find an emotional safe harbour until the skies clear.

# Postscript

# Closing Thoughts

And so we reach the end of this endeavour.

I have attempted to make a case for the moon, the past and for Ishtar, and I hope that you find this, if nothing else, a fun, enlightening reference. Or perhaps you see something more thought-provoking and inspiring in it. Either way, I loved writing it, and I hope you enjoyed it.

While this book is on its final chapter, I feel that I have only just begun to scratch the surface of the connection between the wisdom of the past, intuition, contemporary psychology and the desire for deeper self-awareness.

As my primary source of fascination – the mysteries of the Mesopotamian empire – continues to be unearthed and translated, the treasures of dream interpretation that were lost have been found, brushed off and will shine bright again.

Humans are born pure. We live, love, labour and perhaps lose our true spirit in the dusts of our everyday toil.

I believe that only by reconnecting with your intuition, your psyche, your past and the moon can you continue to excavate the most important treasure of all: yourself.

Much love, Flo x

# Acknowledgements

To my wonderful agent Kizzy, thank you for believing in me and for your ongoing hard work and support. Gratitude to Steve for his wisdom and dedication. Elizabeth for helping with the book cover design. And to the wonderful people at Watkins Media for publishing my book and making this happen. A thank you to Darren and Simon for taking care of auntyflo.com. Love to both my chidren, Owen and Luke, for helping me work on this beautiful book. And, if you are holding this book in your hands, then I am grateful for your support.

# About the Author

Psychic and occult expert Florance Saul is the creator of AuntyFlo.com, the go-to spiritual destination for the most comprehensive guidance on dream meanings and lunar wisdom on the internet. Since its launch, her dream site alone has enjoyed over 100 million visitors, and her Tarot work touches and inspires millions more.

Since the age of eight, Florance has dedicated herself to exploring the spiritual dimension of the human experience and presenting it in an accessible way, guiding millions of loyal readers to greater self-awareness. Having worked in marketing for 20 years, project-managing many TV and Fortune 100 websites, she uses her communications skills to encourage others on their spiritual journey, opening the gateway to the subtle beauty of spirituality that vibrates within us all.

# Index